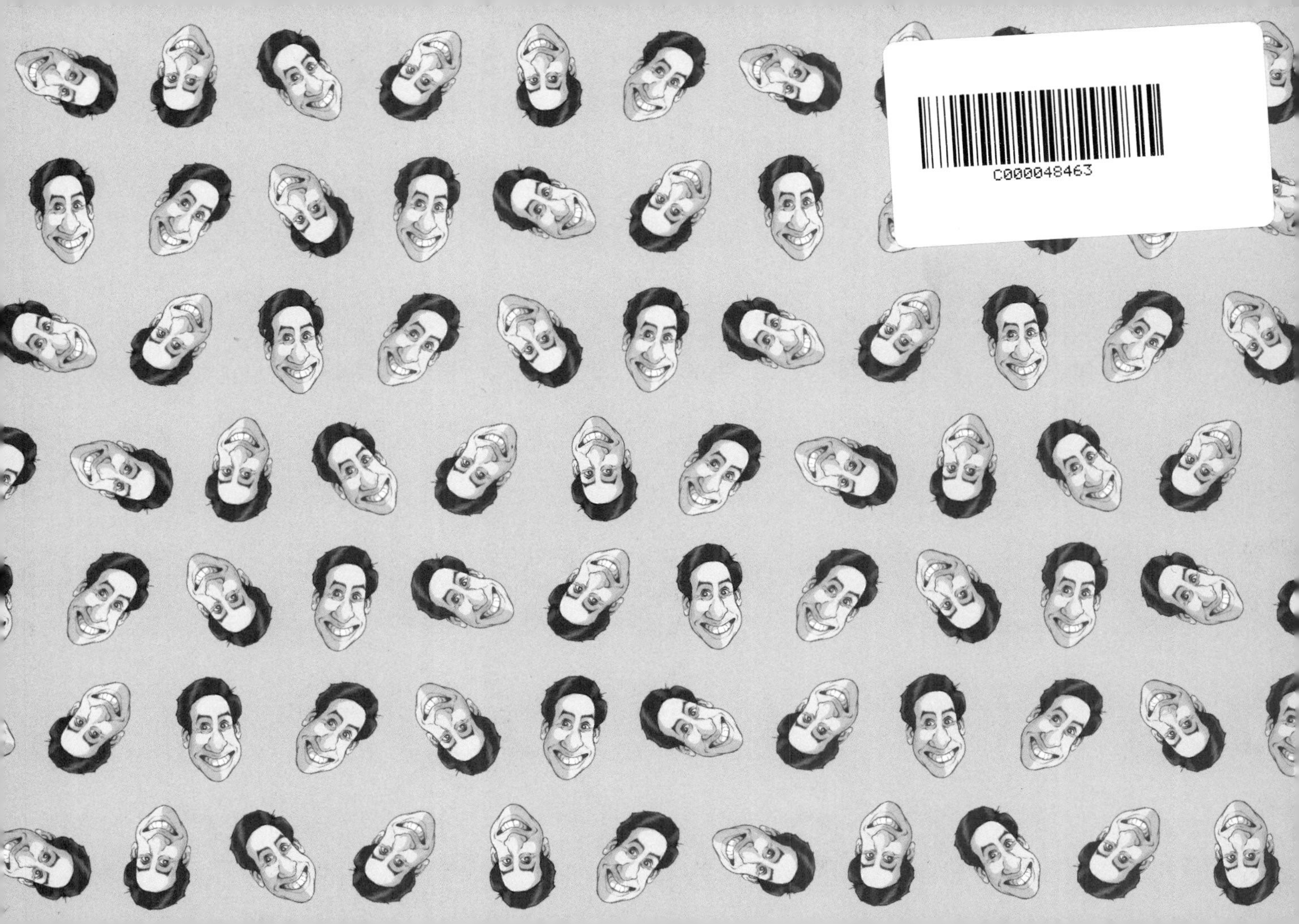

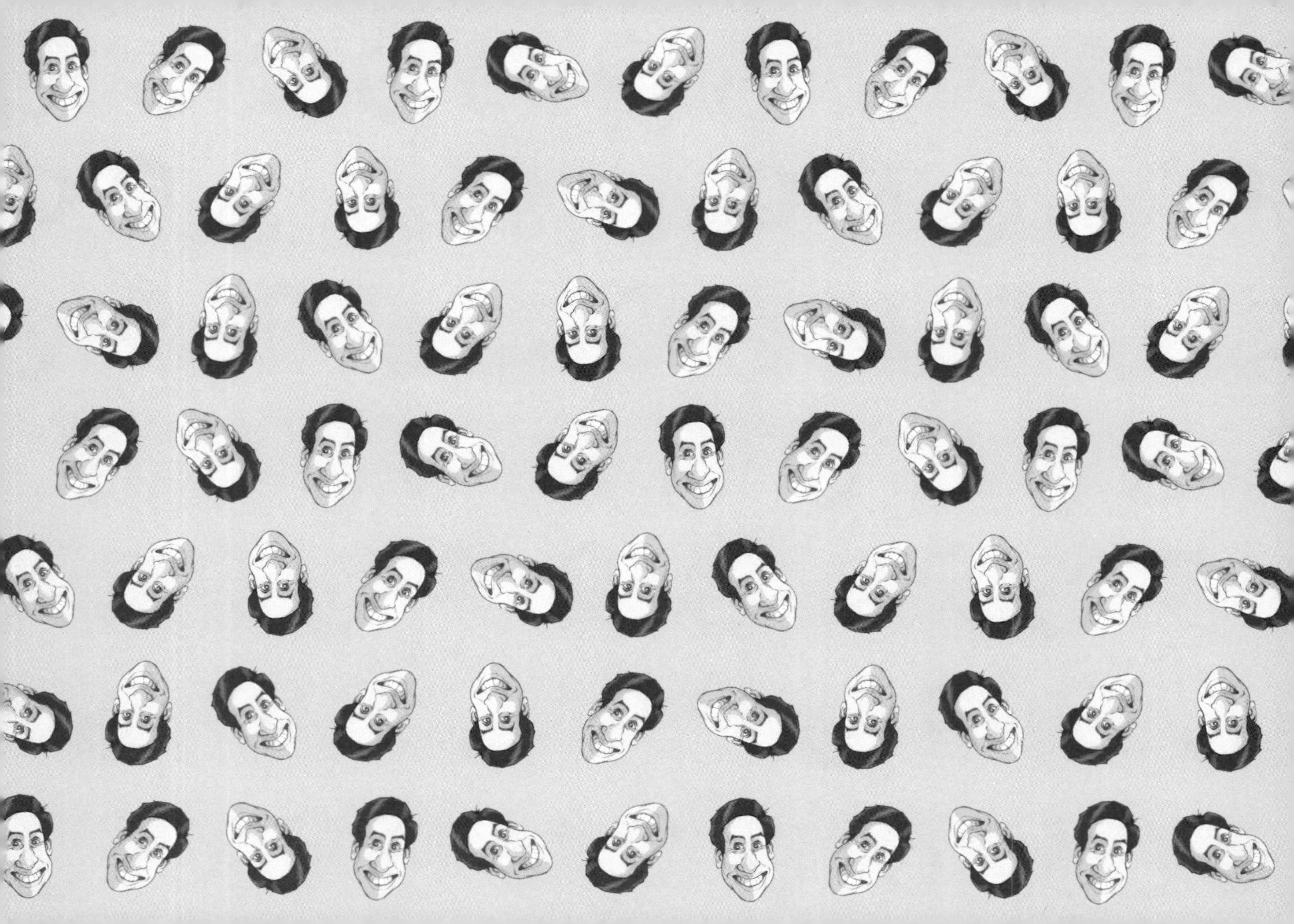

# CHAOS
## WITH
# ED MILIBAND

# CHAOS
## WITH
# ED MILIBAND

**Roger Gammon**

**Illustrated by Milligan**

For David*

*both of them

'Britain faces a simple and inescapable choice – stability and strong government with me, or chaos with Ed Miliband'

**David Cameron, 4 May 2015**

# 7 May 2015

David Cameron (Conservative) defeats Ed Miliband (Labour) in the United Kingdom general election, winning by 330 seats to 232. As Mr Cameron predicted, the following years for the UK were a period of incredible stability, growth and common-sense thinking, with very little bad news to report.

Mr Miliband was not so lucky.

Over the following pages, we follow the main news stories and issues that have arisen since that election, in stark contrast to the turmoil, hardship, and downright anarchy that has occurred in Ed's life.

I'm sure you'll agree, we can all be very thankful that Mr Cameron helped secure this period of 'stability and strong government', and that we were all spared from what can only be described as ***chaos with Ed Miliband***…

**14 August 2015**
Ballot papers are sent out as the voting process begins to elect a new Leader of the Labour Party, following Ed's resignation. The four candidates are Andy Burnham, Yvette Cooper, Liz Kendall and Jeremy Corbyn.

**TODAY ED MILIBAND...**
walked to the local park to feed some stale bread to the ducks;
got pecked several times by an overly-aggressive swan.

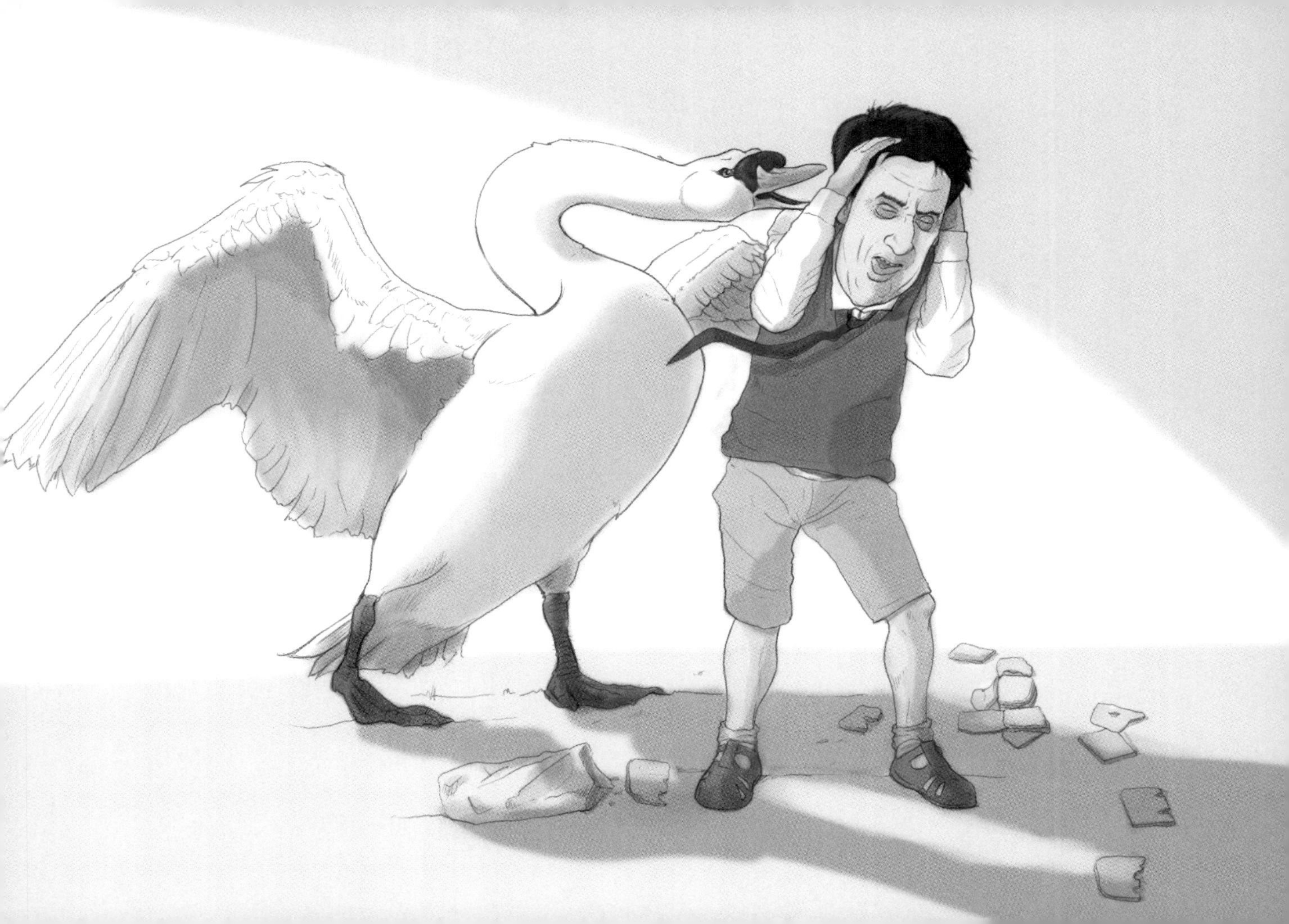

**12 September 2015**
Jeremy Corbyn is appointed Leader of the Labour Party and Leader of the Opposition in a landslide victory, with 59.5% of first-preference votes.


**TODAY ED MILIBAND...**
drove approx. 43 miles each way to a model village
so he could pretend to be a giant.

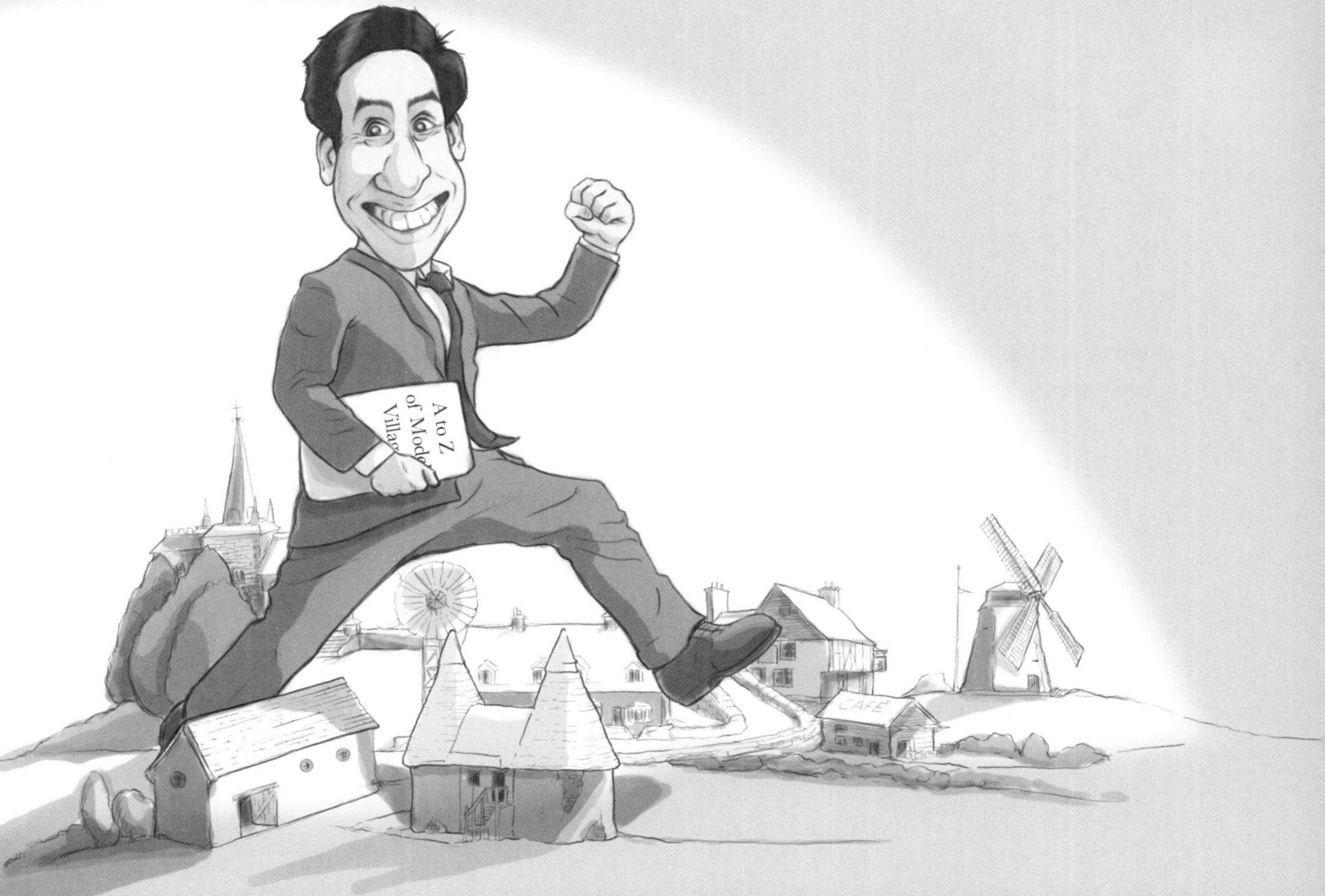
A to Z
CAFÉ

**19 February 2016**
Prime Minister David Cameron secures a deal with EU leaders, including powers to limit some EU migrants' benefits, and describes it as giving the UK 'special status'.

**TODAY ED MILIBAND...**
batch cooked three pots of vegan chilli and shared it all with his neighbours.

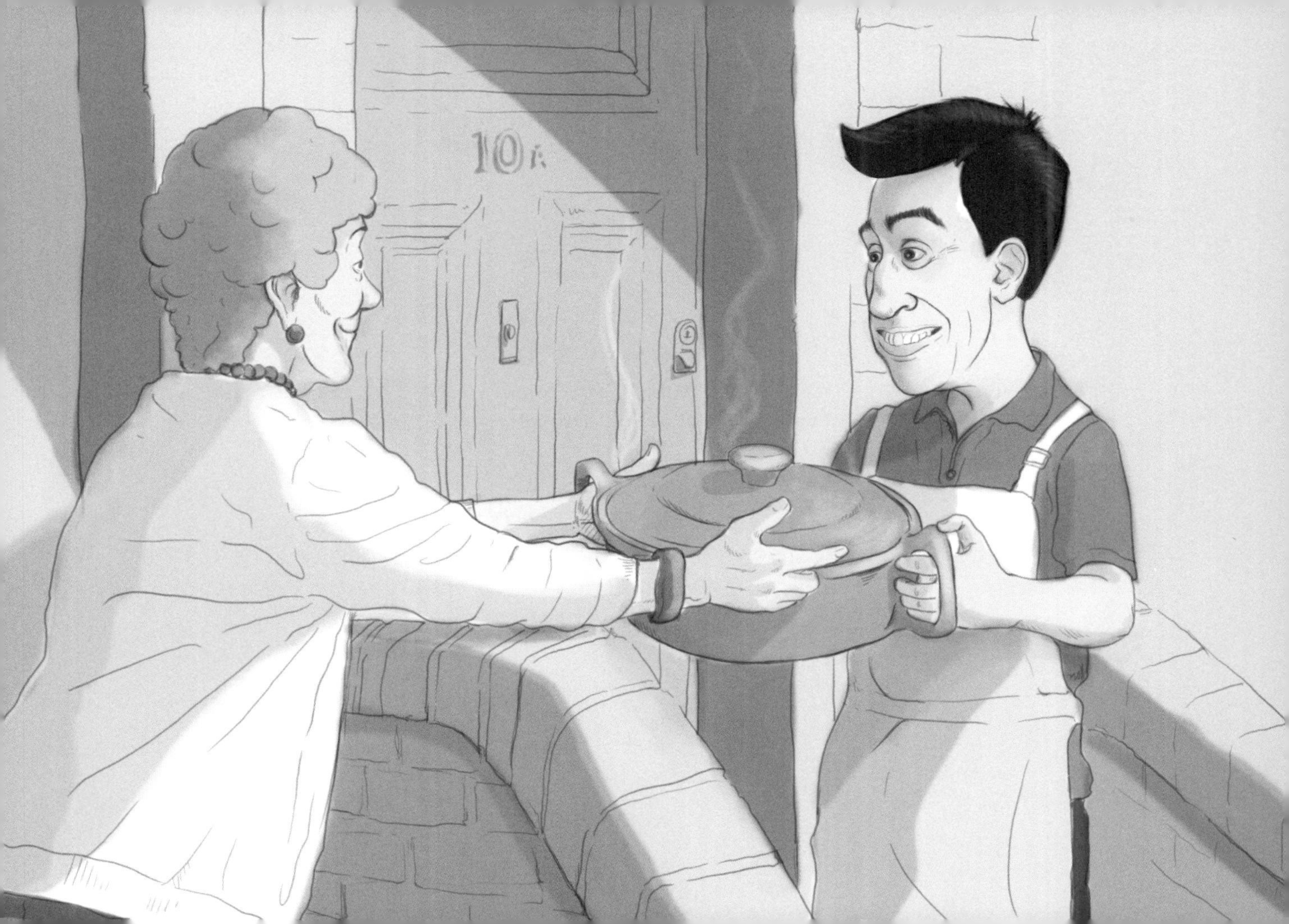
10

**20 February 2016**
Prime Minister David Cameron sets the referendum date to vote on whether
the UK will remain in the EU: Thursday, 23 June 2016.


**TODAY ED MILIBAND...**
realised he'd accidentally given away the extra portion of vegan chilli he'd saved
for his tea, and had to make do with some leftover celery and a boiled egg.

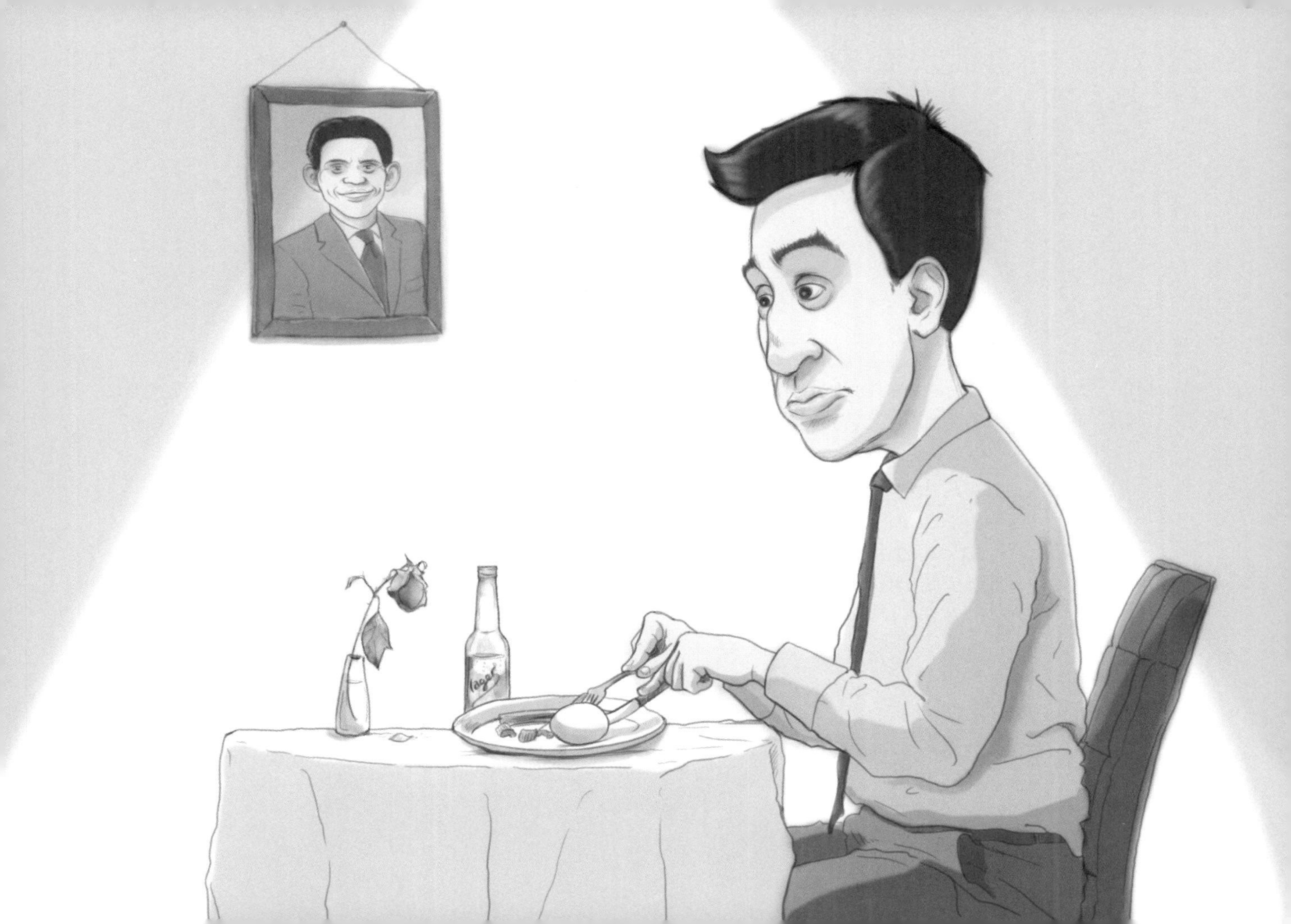
lager

**18 April 2016**
HM Treasury releases its analysis on the impact of leaving the EU, predicting that the UK will be worse off by £4,300 a year per household if the country votes to leave.

**TODAY ED MILIBAND...**
took his small change collection to the coin machine in Asda for his annual 'big count', donating the full £212.72 to a local owl sanctuary.

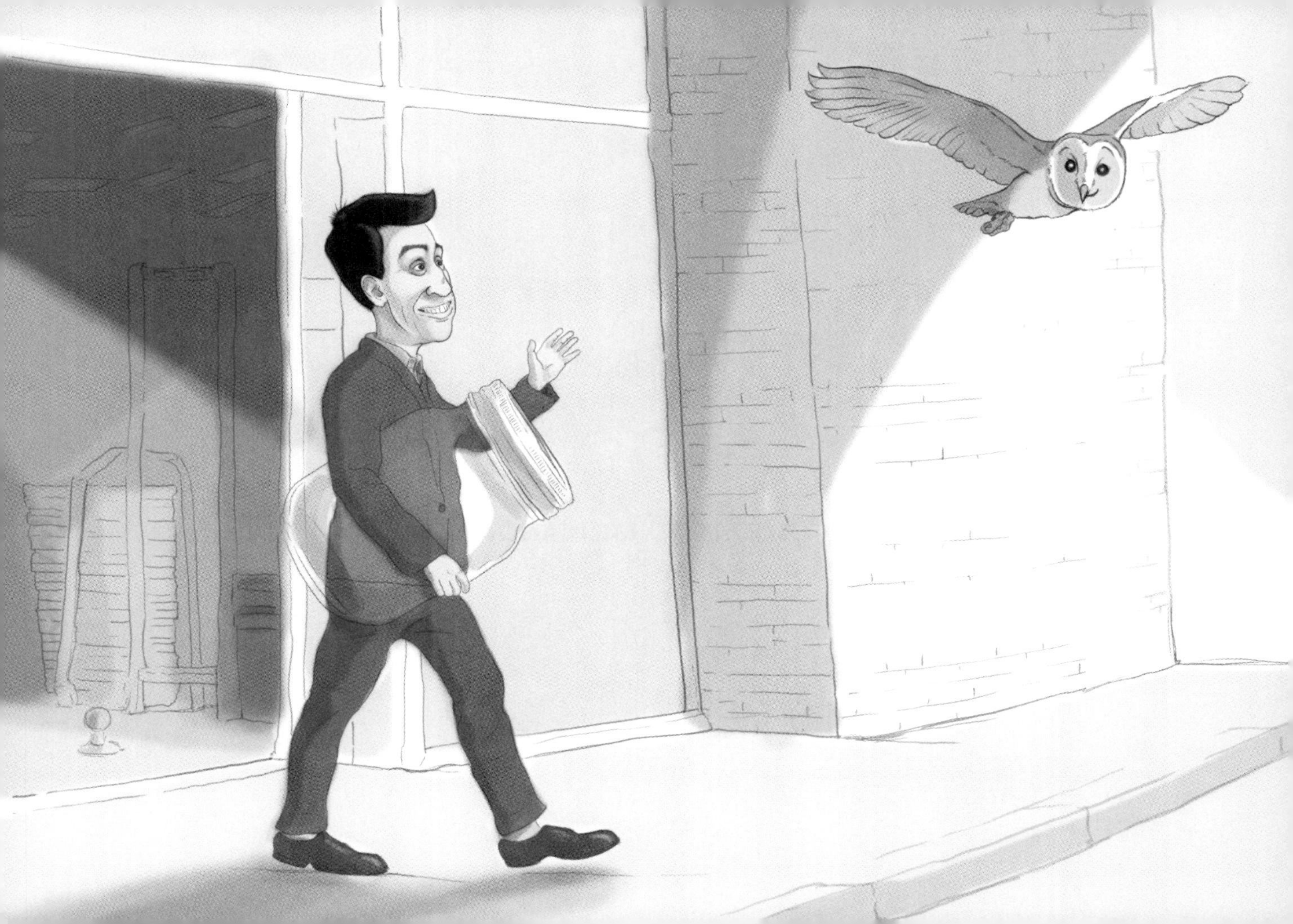

**22 April 2016**
On a visit to London, President Barack Obama warns that leaving the EU will put the UK at the 'back of the queue' for any trade deal talks with the US.

**TODAY ED MILIBAND...**
returned his overdue books to the library (£1.22 fine, paid in full).

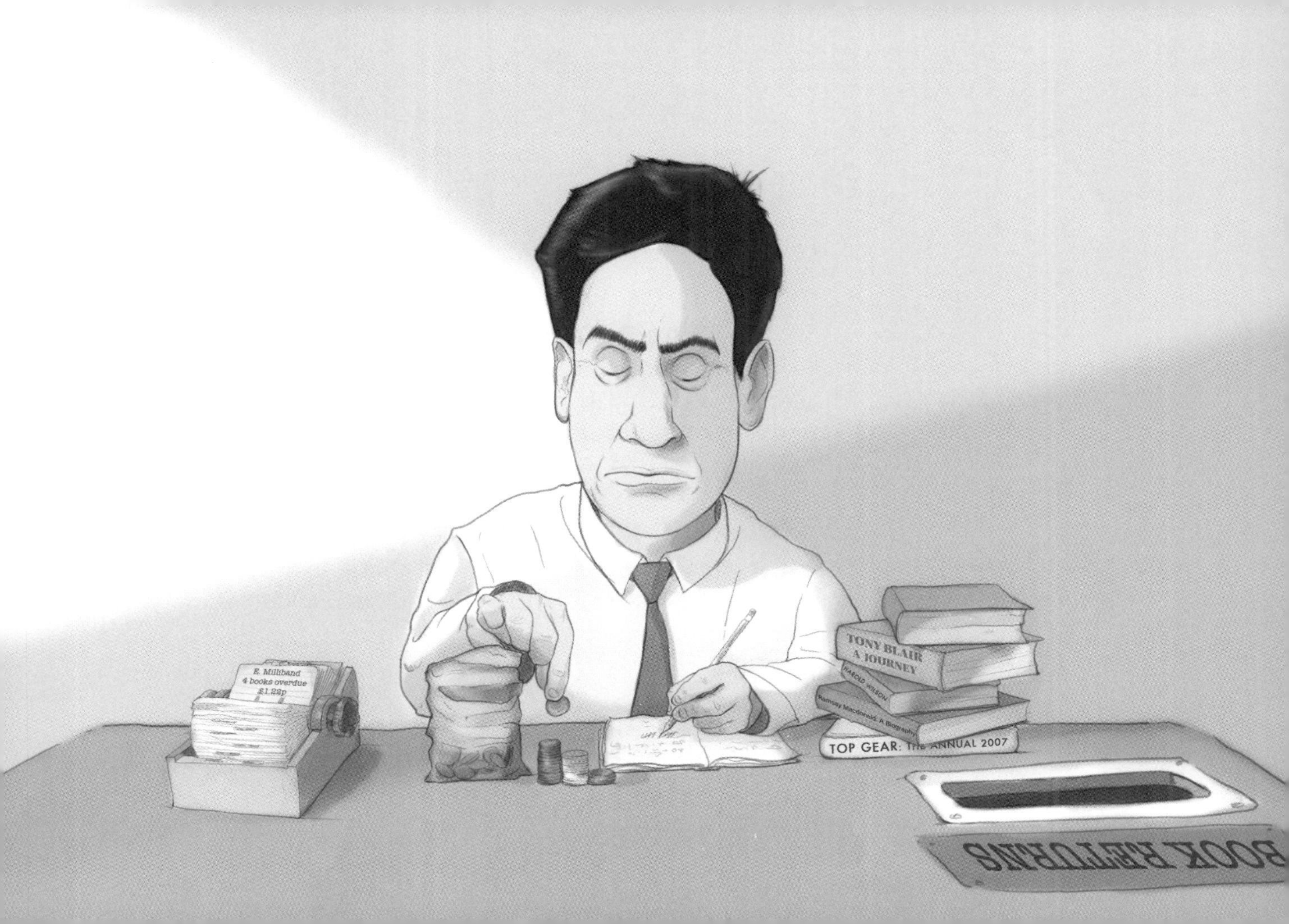
E. Milliband
4 books overdue
£1.22p
TONY BLAIR
A JOURNEY
HAROLD WILSON
Ramsay Macdonald: A Biography
TOP GEAR: THE ANNUAL 2007
BOOK RETURNS

**25 April 2016**
In a speech at the Institue of Mechanical Engineers in London, Home Secretary Theresa May says, 'I believe it is clearly in our national interest to remain a member of the European Union'.


**TODAY ED MILIBAND...**
decided to take up vaping. Not a fan of the sweet taste, he couldn't help but wonder why there's no bacon sandwich flavour on the market. Possible start-up?

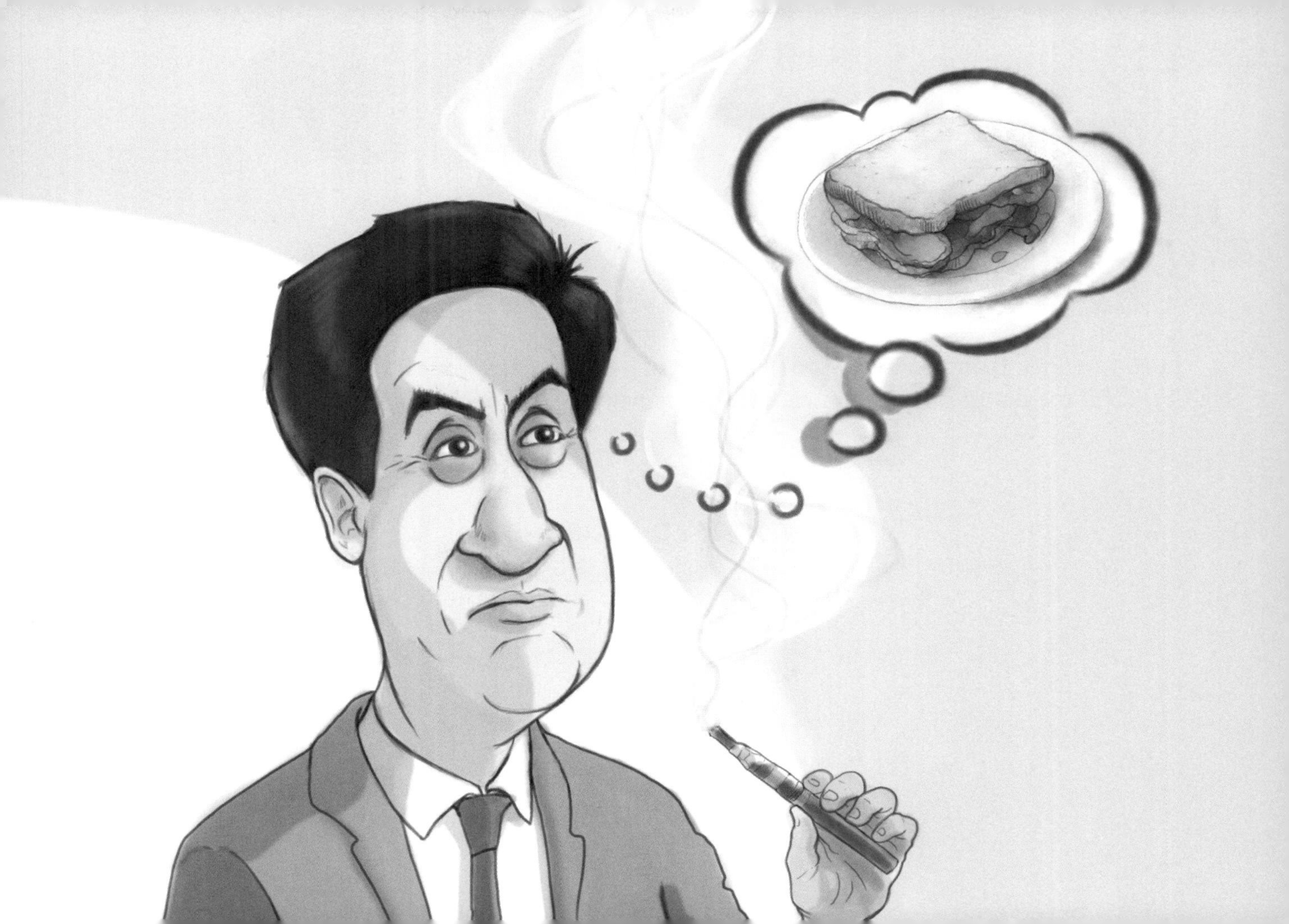

**11 May 2016**
In Truro, Boris Johnson boards the Vote Leave campaign bus for the first time. The message on the bus reads: 'We send the EU £350 million a week, let's fund our NHS instead'.


**TODAY ED MILIBAND...**
added seven more locations (plus facilities checklist) to his 'Service Stations of the UK' master spreadsheet.

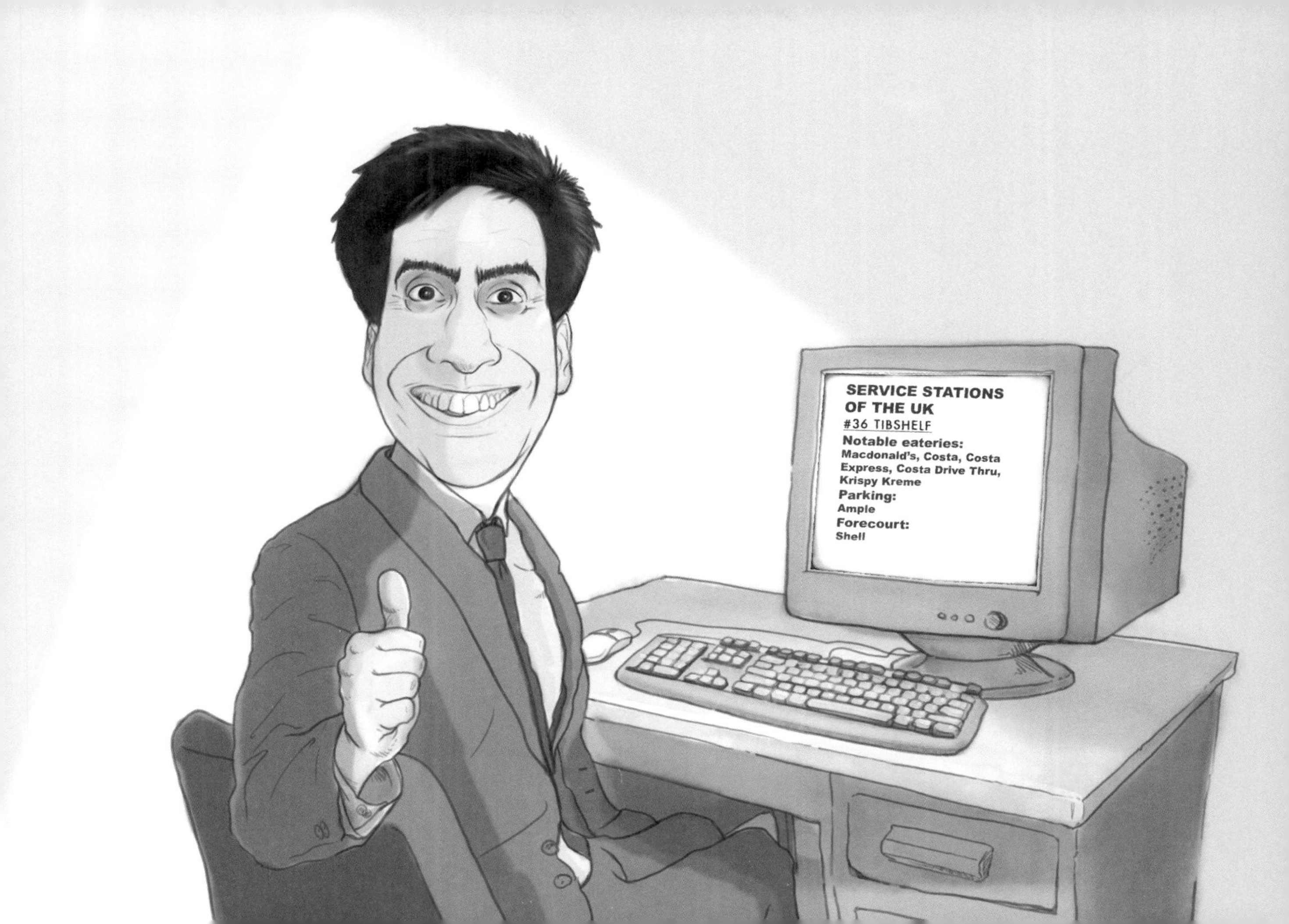
SERVICE STATIONS
OF THE UK
#36 TIBSHELF
Notable eateries:
Macdonald's, Costa, Costa Express, Costa Drive Thru, Krispy Kreme
Parking:
Ample
Forecourt:
Shell

**15 June 2016**
Nigel Farage and Bob Geldof's rival referendum flotillas clash on the River Thames,
as they trade insults and spray each other with water.


**TODAY ED MILIBAND...**
drank espresso at 9.39 p.m. at a dinner party to be polite; was still awake at 2.13 a.m.

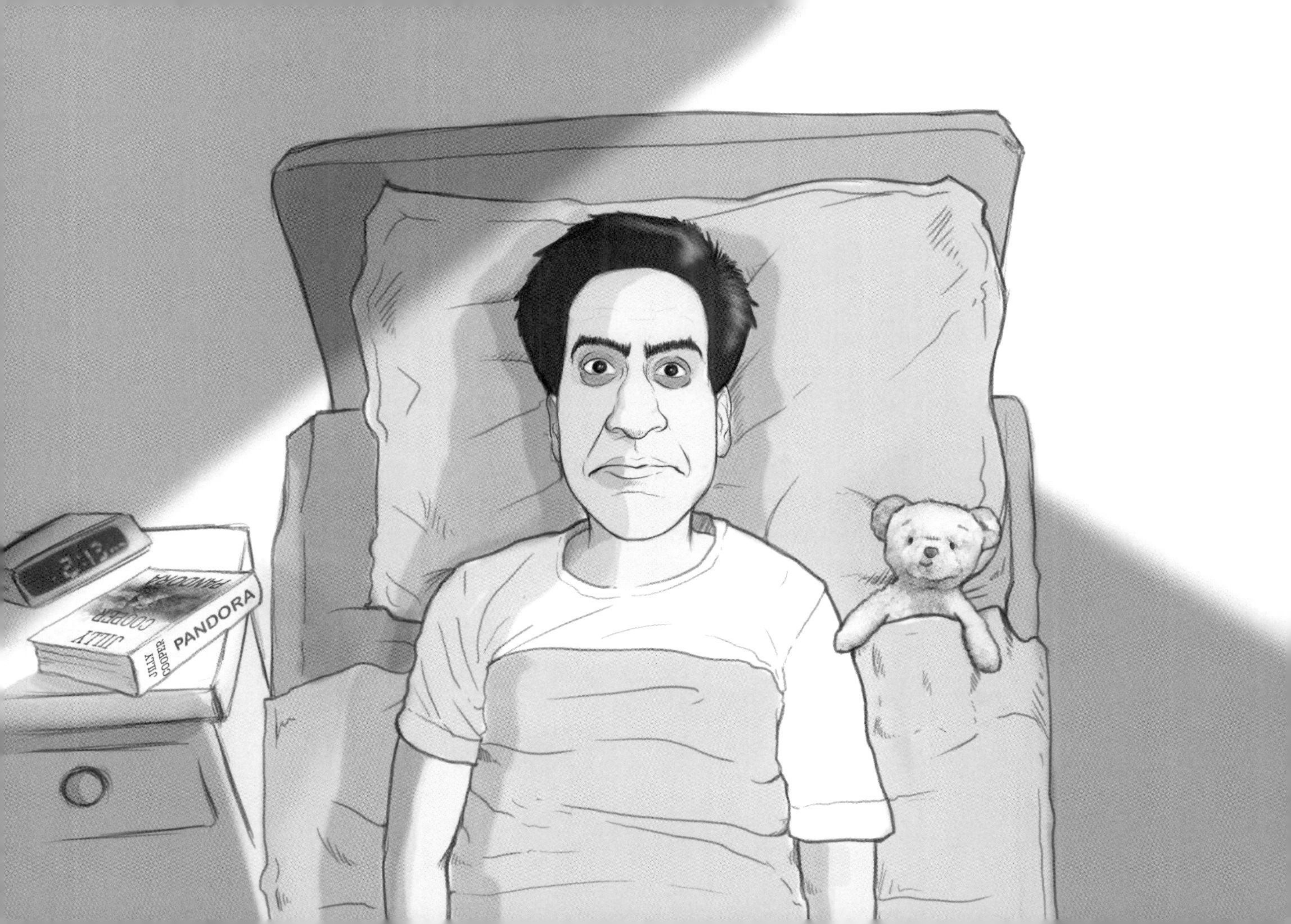
JILLY COOPER
PANDORA

**23 June 2016**
Britain goes to the polls to vote in the EU referendum.
Leave wins with 51.89% of the vote.

## TODAY ED MILIBAND...
decided to get away from it all. After casting his vote, he went to a midweek meetup for a New Forest-based medieval reenactment group, the Southampton Siege Society. Three invasion scenarios and one multiman skirmish, followed by a ploughman's at The Hound and Badger, all before driving back home to watch the Remain victory unfold. Bliss.

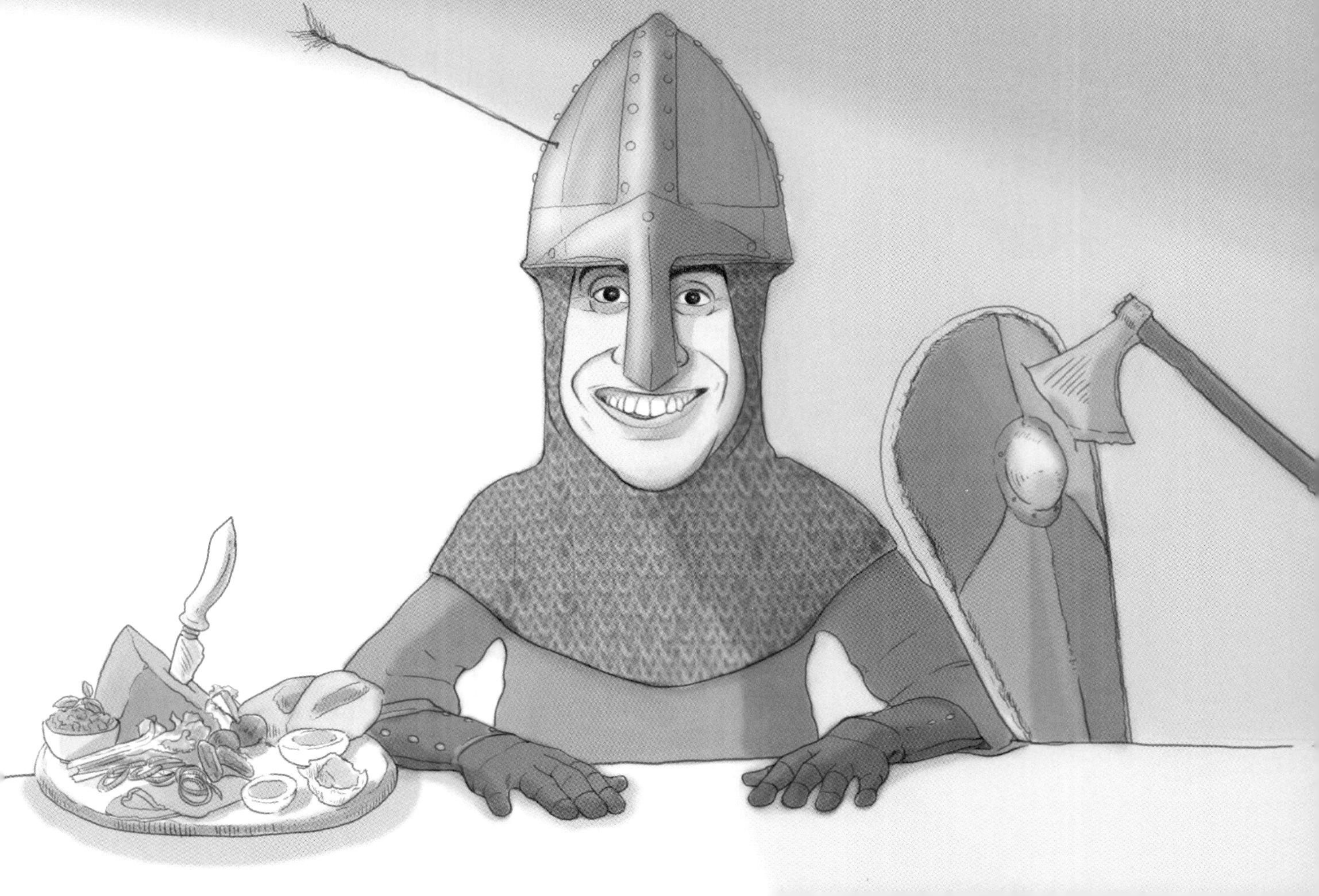

**24 June 2016**
Prime Minister David Cameron announces his resignation following the referendum result.


**TODAY ED MILIBAND...**
closed the curtains, turned off his phone, brought his duvet down to the sofa and watched the first three *Toy Story* films back-to-back ('that scene in the furnace gets me every time'). Total ice cream consumption: 500ml triple choc chip.

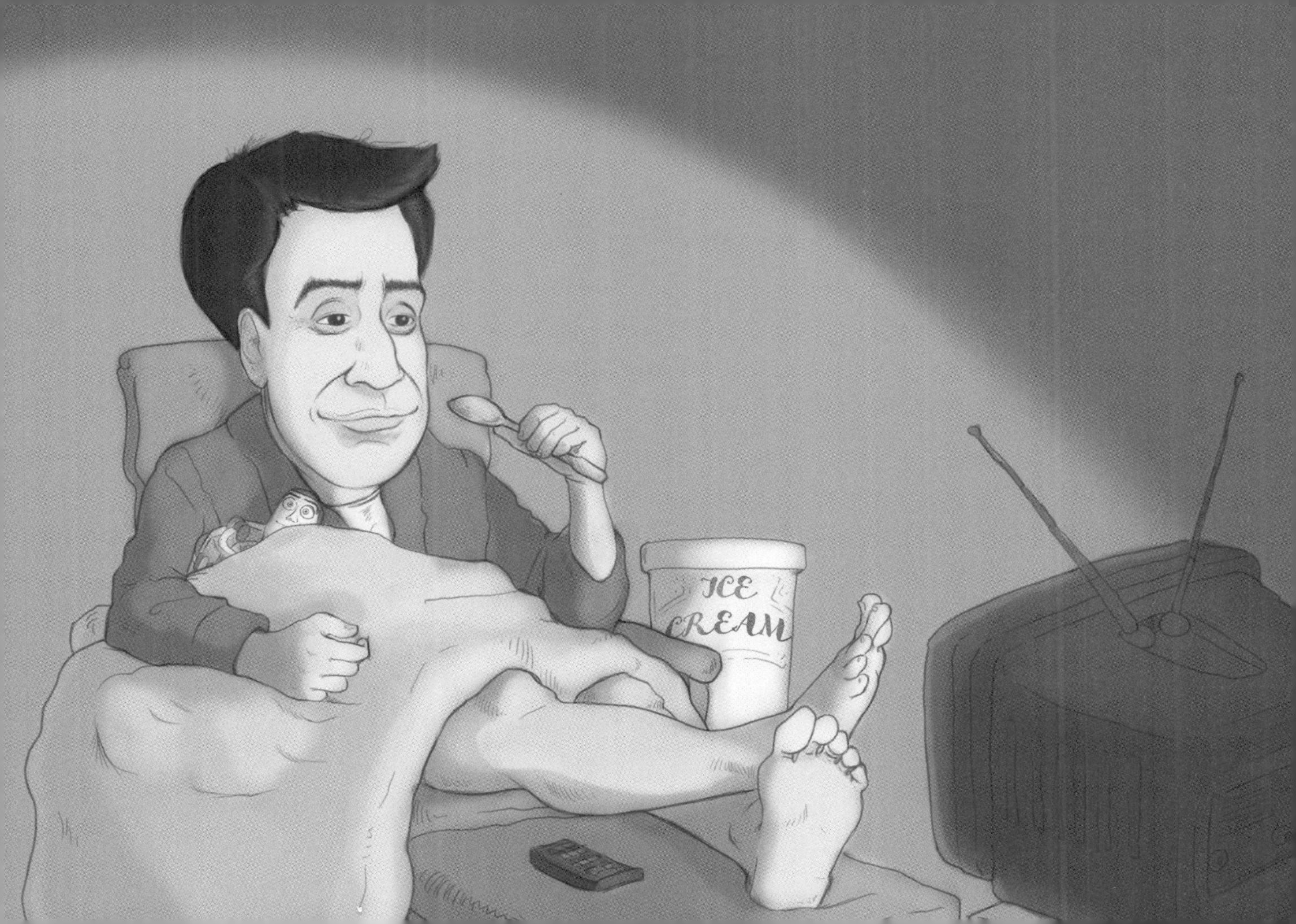
ICE CREAM

**11 July 2016**
After Andrea Leadsom, the only other remaining candidate, withdraws from the election, Theresa May is named the new Leader of the Conservative Party.


**TODAY ED MILIBAND...**
finally finished his 10,000 piece jigsaw ('The Lighthouse Keeper's Retreat').

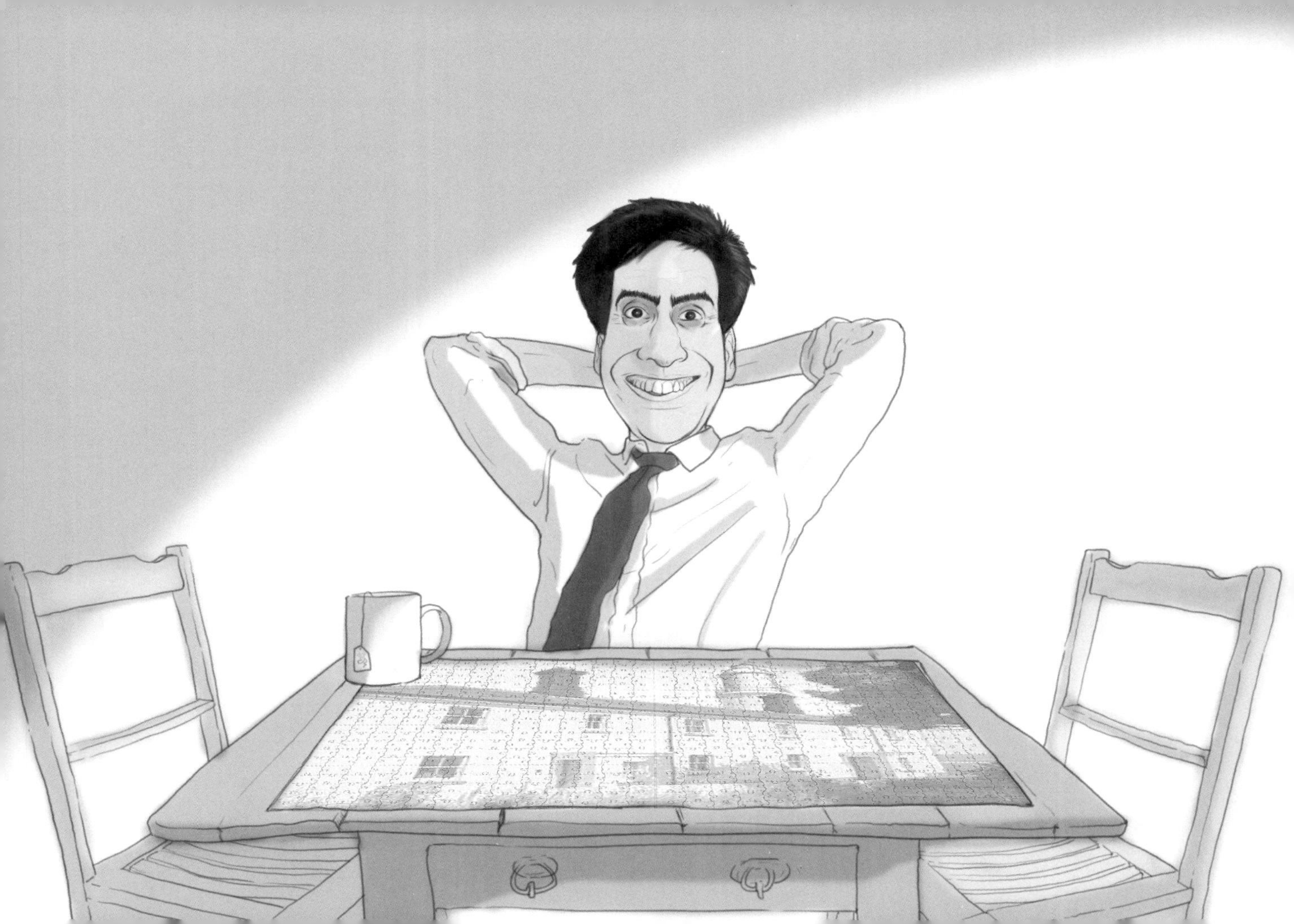

**13 July 2016**
Theresa May is appointed Prime Minister by Queen Elizabeth II.
David Davis is appointed Secretary of State for Exiting the European Union.


**TODAY ED MILIBAND…**
rose above last year's card snub from his brother – cards don't get lost in the post
these days, and *certainly* not three years running – and posted David's birthday card
(watercolour cricket pitch scene) and gift (*The Best of Time Team* eleven-DVD box set).

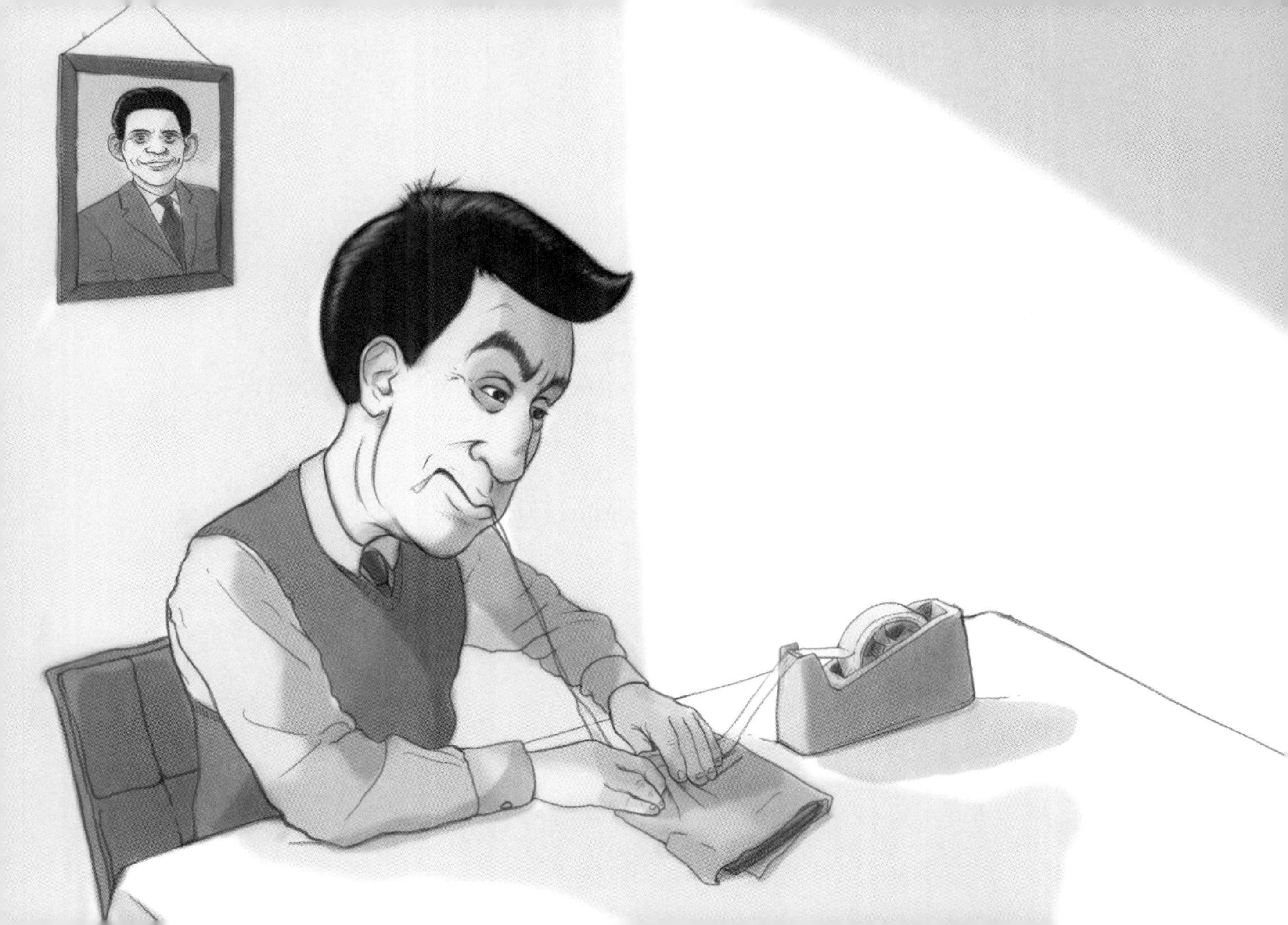

**24 September 2016**
Jeremy Corbyn defeats Owen Smith in the Labour Party leadership election, increasing his share of the vote from 59.5% to 61.8% compared with the 2015 result.

**TODAY ED MILIBAND...**
performed his annual sock drawer audit. Four pairs successfully re-matched, seven sorry singles binned and one damaged walking sock darned back to full fitness. Result!

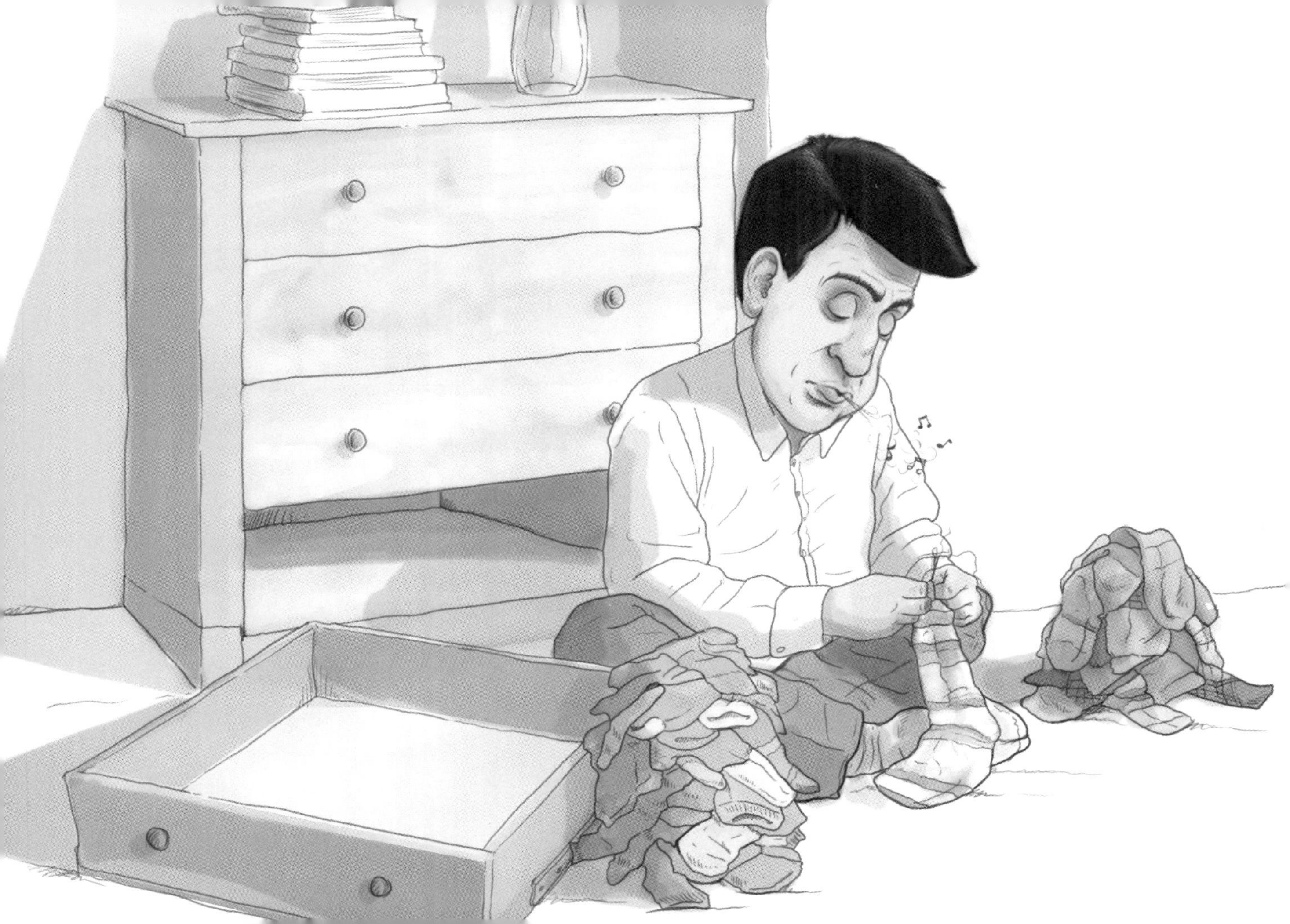

**2 October 2016**

Prime Minister Theresa May confirms that Article 50 will be triggered at the end of March 2017, marking the start of a two-year exit process and meaning the UK will have left the EU by summer 2019.

**TODAY ED MILIBAND...**

rescued a kitten from a tree. Or helped, anyway. Pride of Britain award incoming?

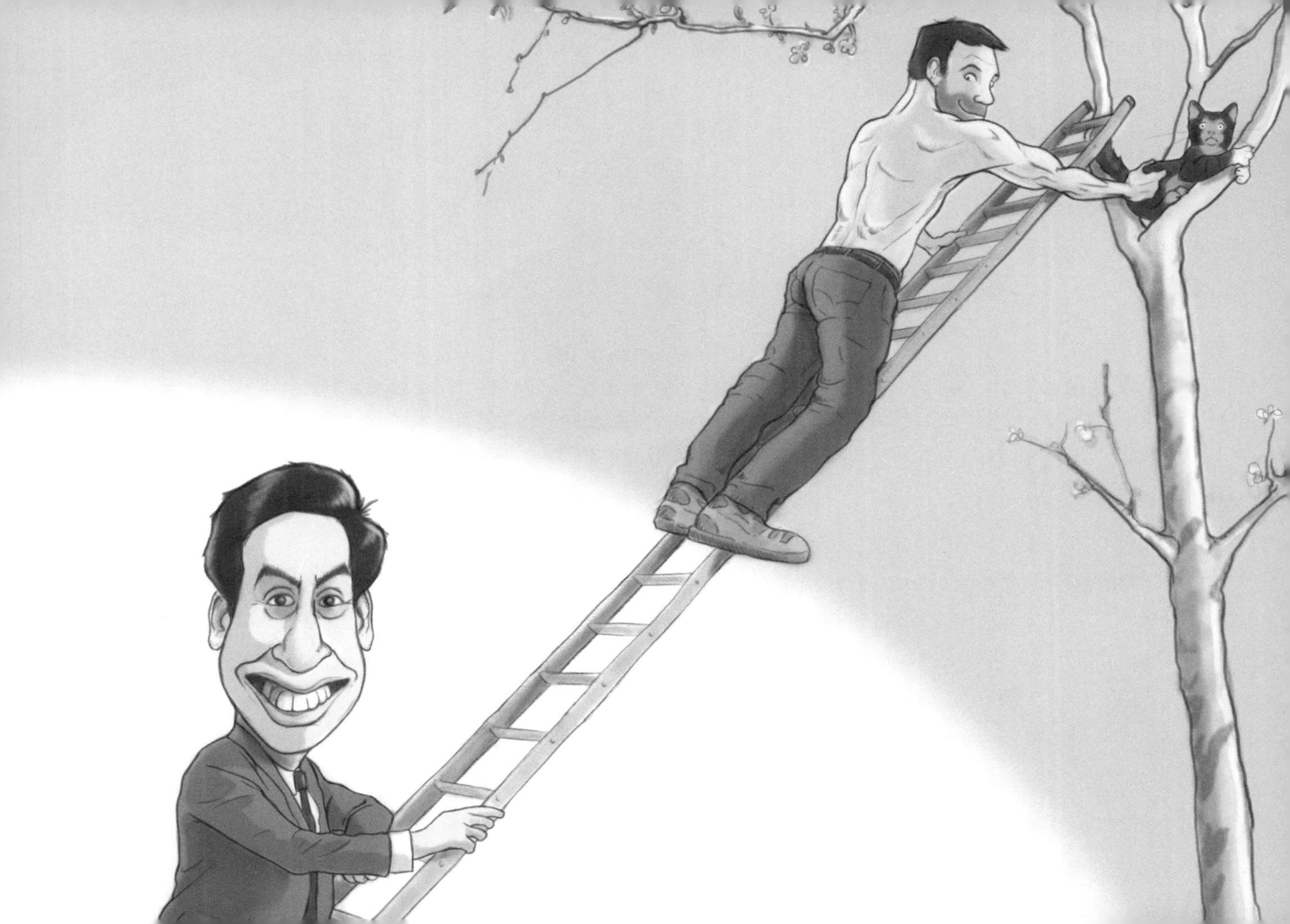

**3 November 2016**
A campaign led by Gina Miller defeats the UK government in a High Court case,
meaning Parliament must vote on whether the UK can start the process of
leaving the EU.


**TODAY ED MILIBAND...**
started writing a historical military novel (working title: *The Brigadier's Last Stand*);
309 words completed.

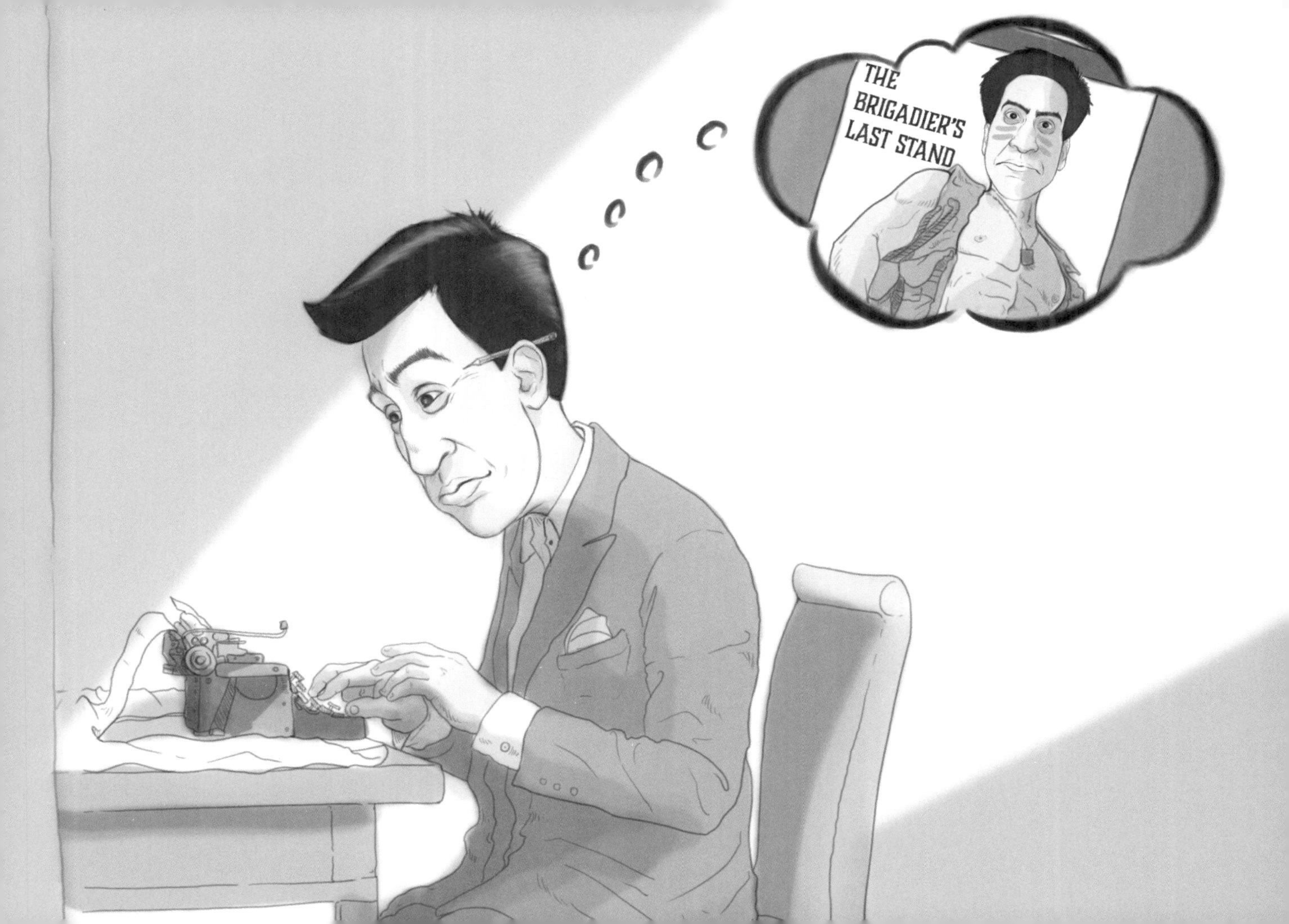
THE BRIGADIER'S LAST STAND

**17 January 2017**
In a speech at Lancaster House, Prime Minister Theresa May sets out the government's 'Plan for Britain' and her Brexit objectives. Key points include leaving the single market and the EU's customs union.

**TODAY ED MILIBAND...**
went all-in with his Christmas money and ordered a unicycle from eBay.

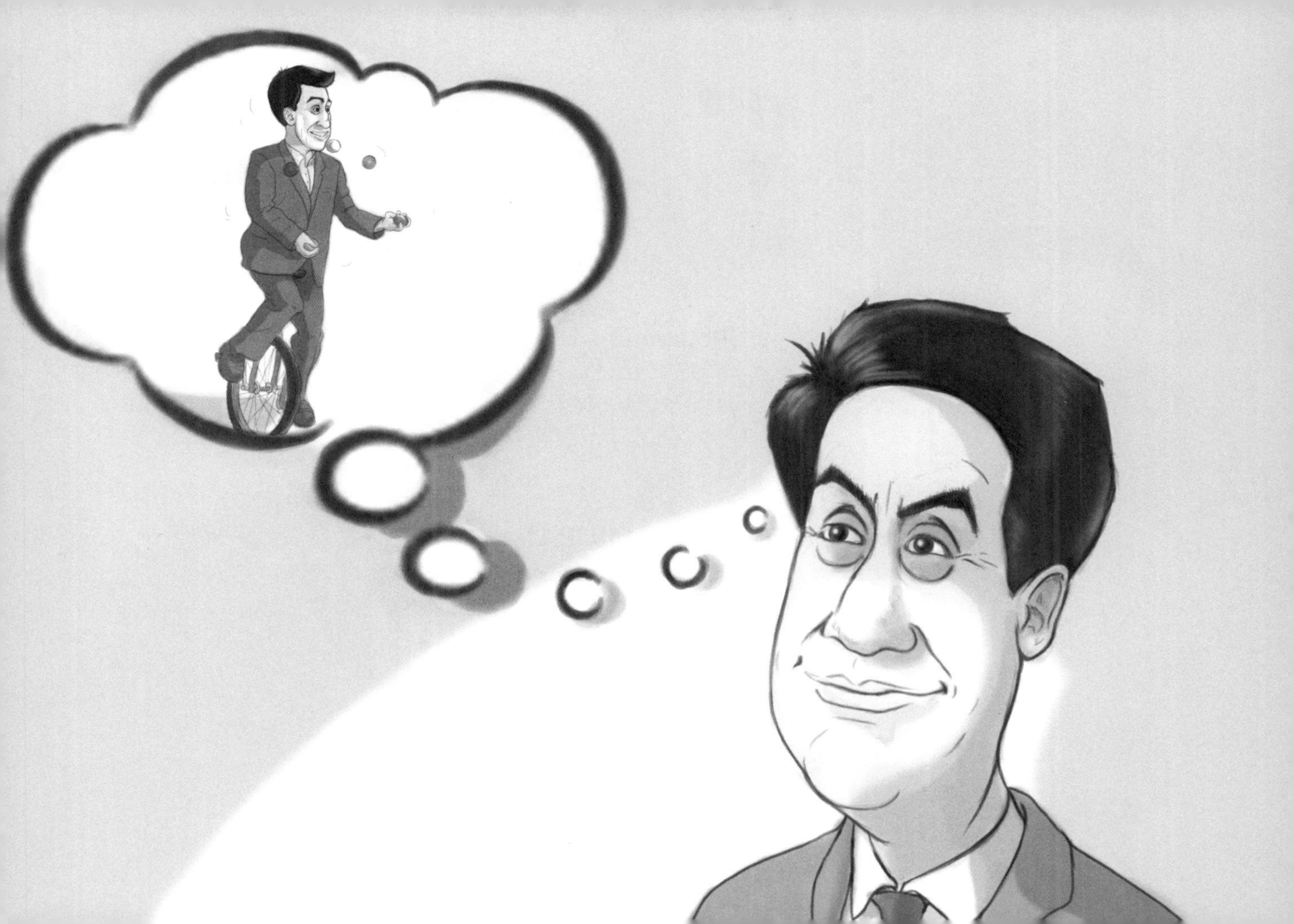

**29 January 2017**
Prime Minister Theresa May meets US President Donald Trump at the White House.
They hold hands, and Trump says that 'Brexit is going to be a wonderful thing for
your country'.


**TODAY ED MILIBAND...**
suffered minor grazes and two bruised knees after falling off his unicycle.
Nothing that a generous smear of antiseptic can't fix, mind.

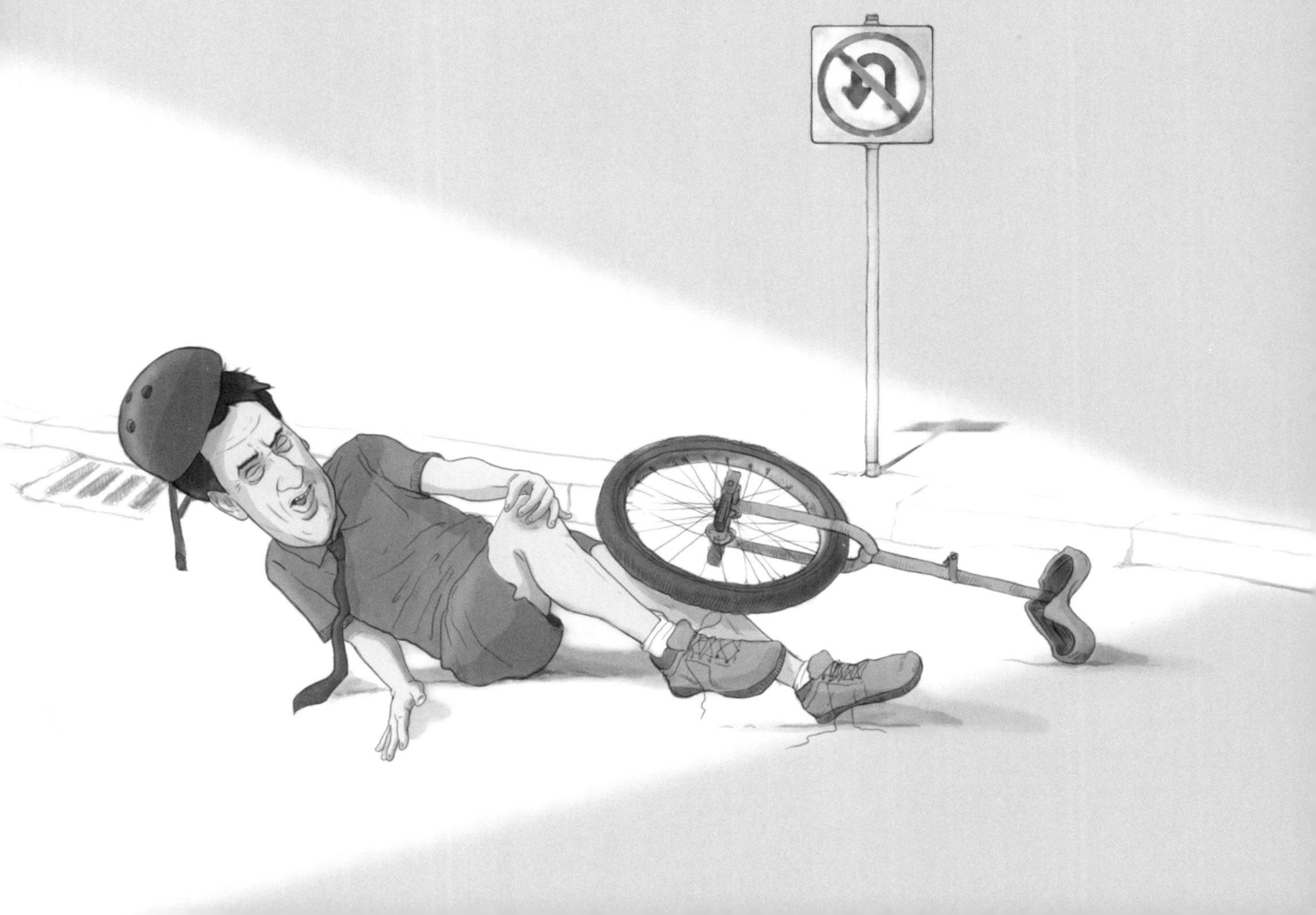

**2 February 2017**
The government publishes its Brexit White Paper, formally setting out its
strategy and twelve principles for the UK to leave the EU.


**TODAY ED MILIBAND...**
finally smashed his top score on the Sudoku app (difficulty level: extreme).

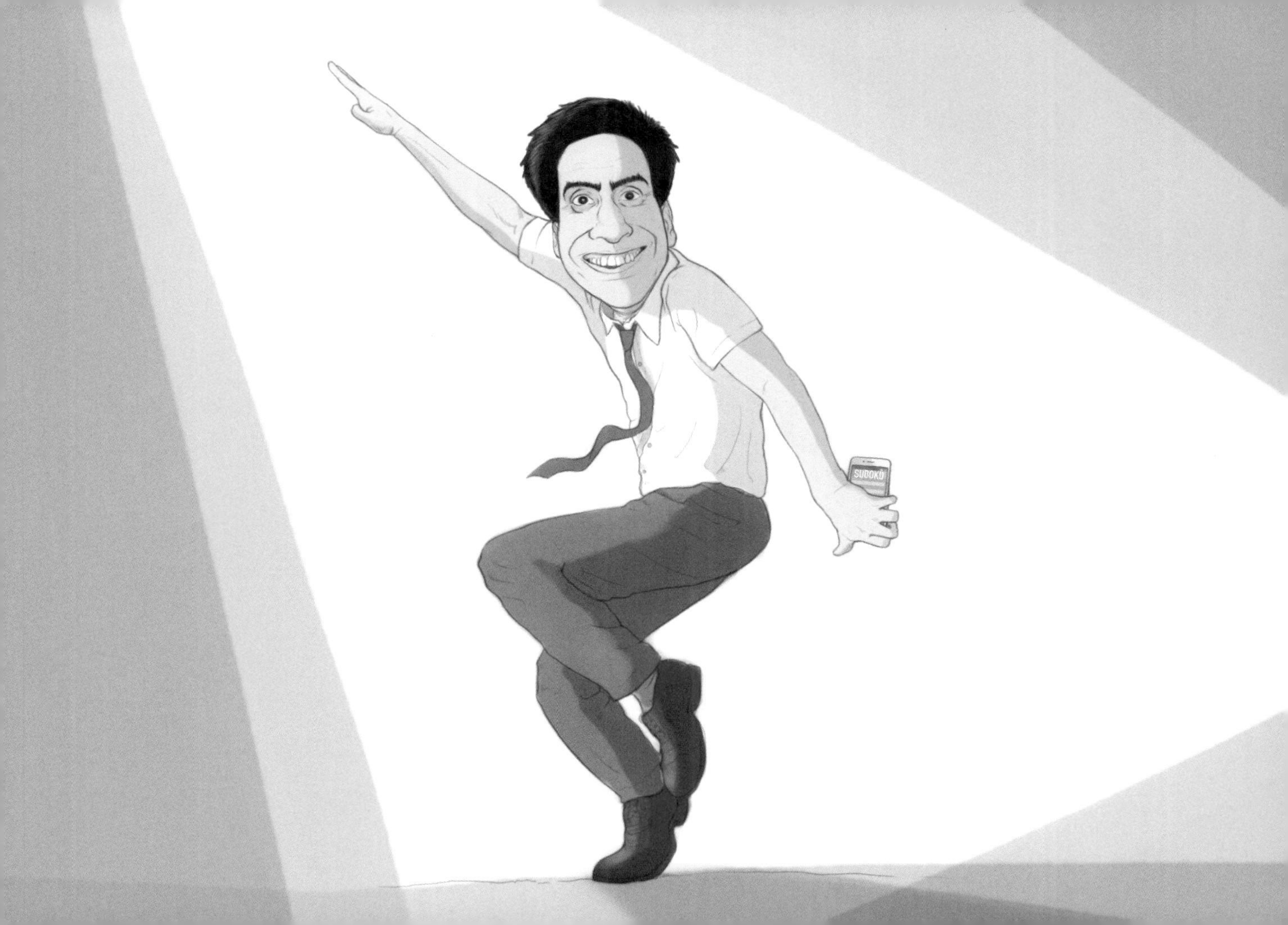
SUDOKU

**18 April 2017**
Prime Minister Theresa May announces a snap general election, to be held on 8 June 2017, in order to secure a parliamentary majority for her Brexit vision.

**TODAY ED MILIBAND…**
ate four bananas back-to-back, then felt a little bit sick for an hour or so.

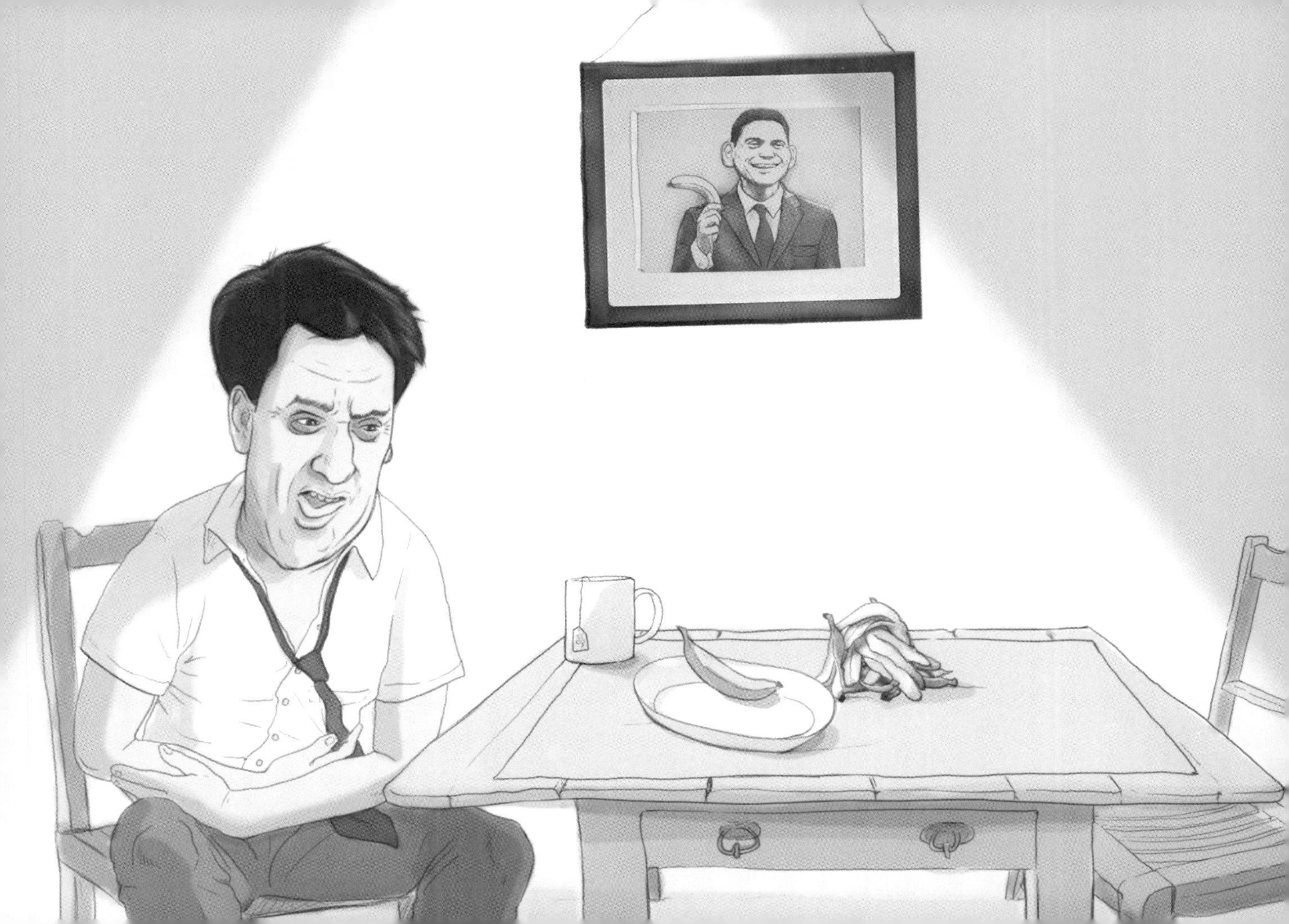

**19 April 2017**
The *Daily Mail* front page headline claims that Mrs May's snap election will
'crush the saboteurs'.


**TODAY ED MILIBAND...**
crushed his enemies... in an online chess tournament.

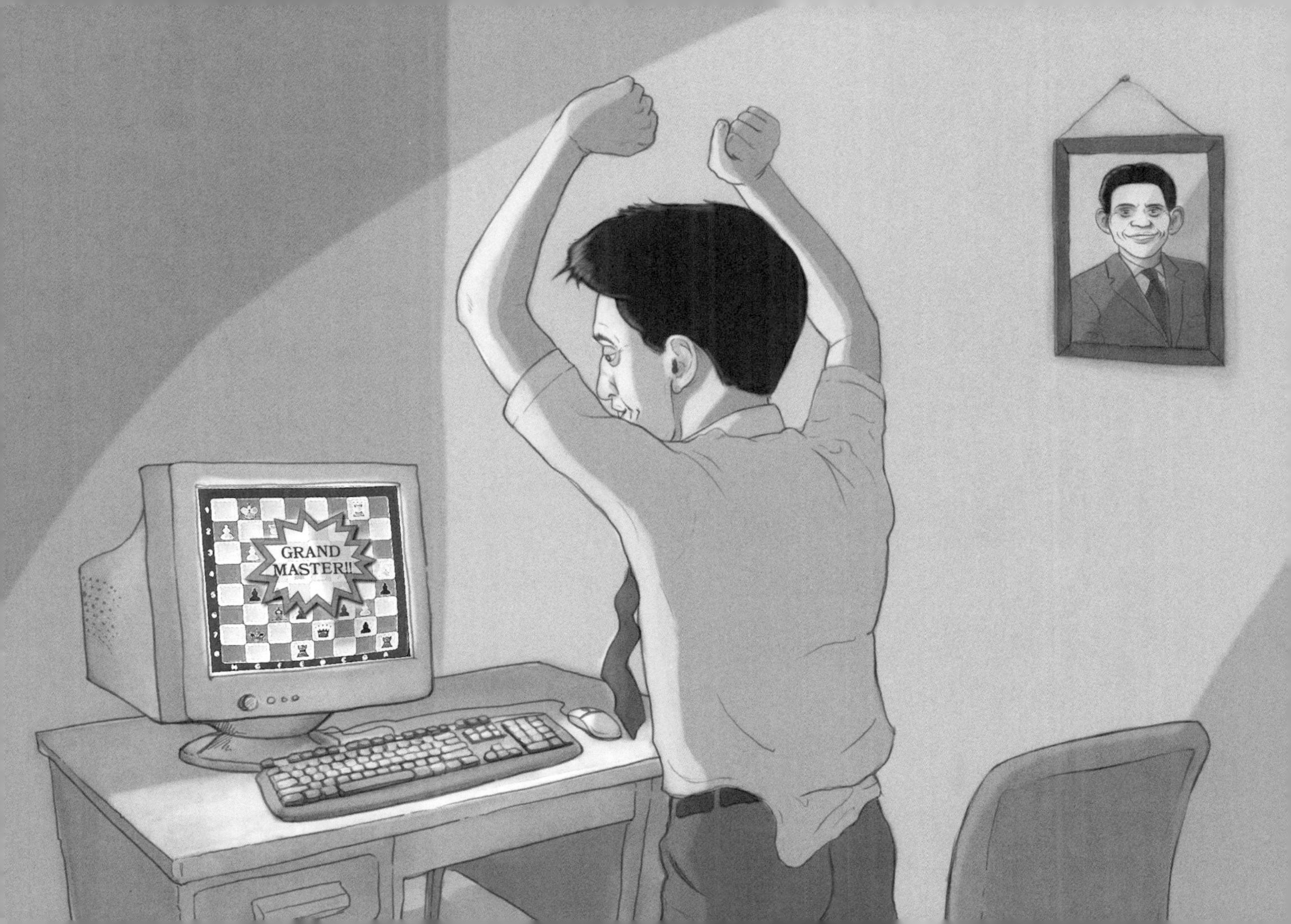
GRAND
MASTER!!

**8 June 2017**
Prime Minister Theresa May loses her parliamentary majority in the general election, as the Conservatives lose thirteen seats. Labour gains thirty seats.


**TODAY ED MILIBAND...**
finally decided on his definitive top three A-ha songs, in order:
3) 'Hunting High and Low'
2) 'Stay on These Roads'
1) 'Take on Me'

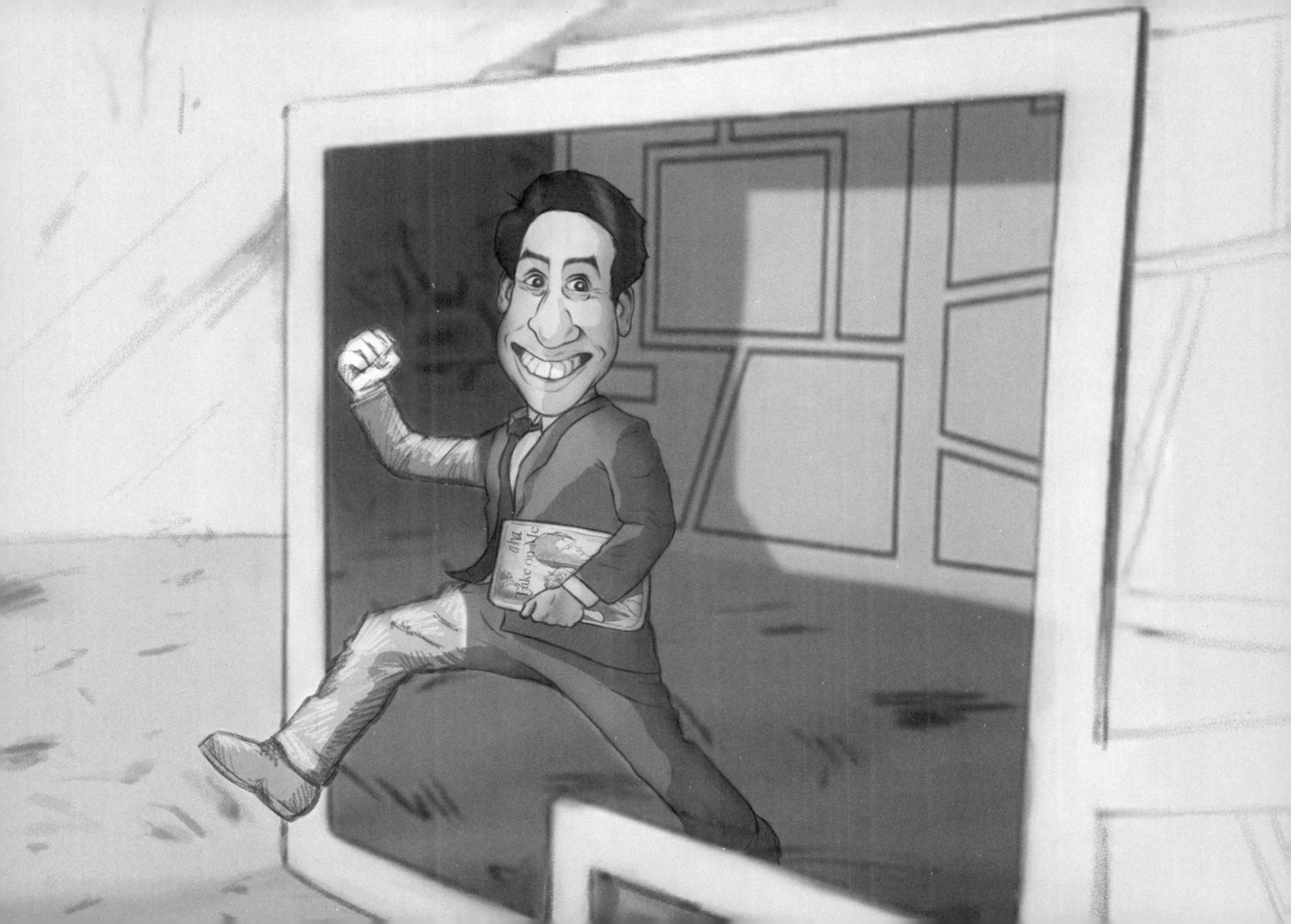
aha
Take on Me

**19 June 2017**
Day one of Brexit negotiation talks begin between the UK and the EU.


**TODAY ED MILIBAND…**
guest hosted his first show on BBC Radio 2. Tracks played included 'One Last Time' by Ariana Grande, 'Radio Ga Ga' by Queen and, of course, A-ha's 'Take On Me'.

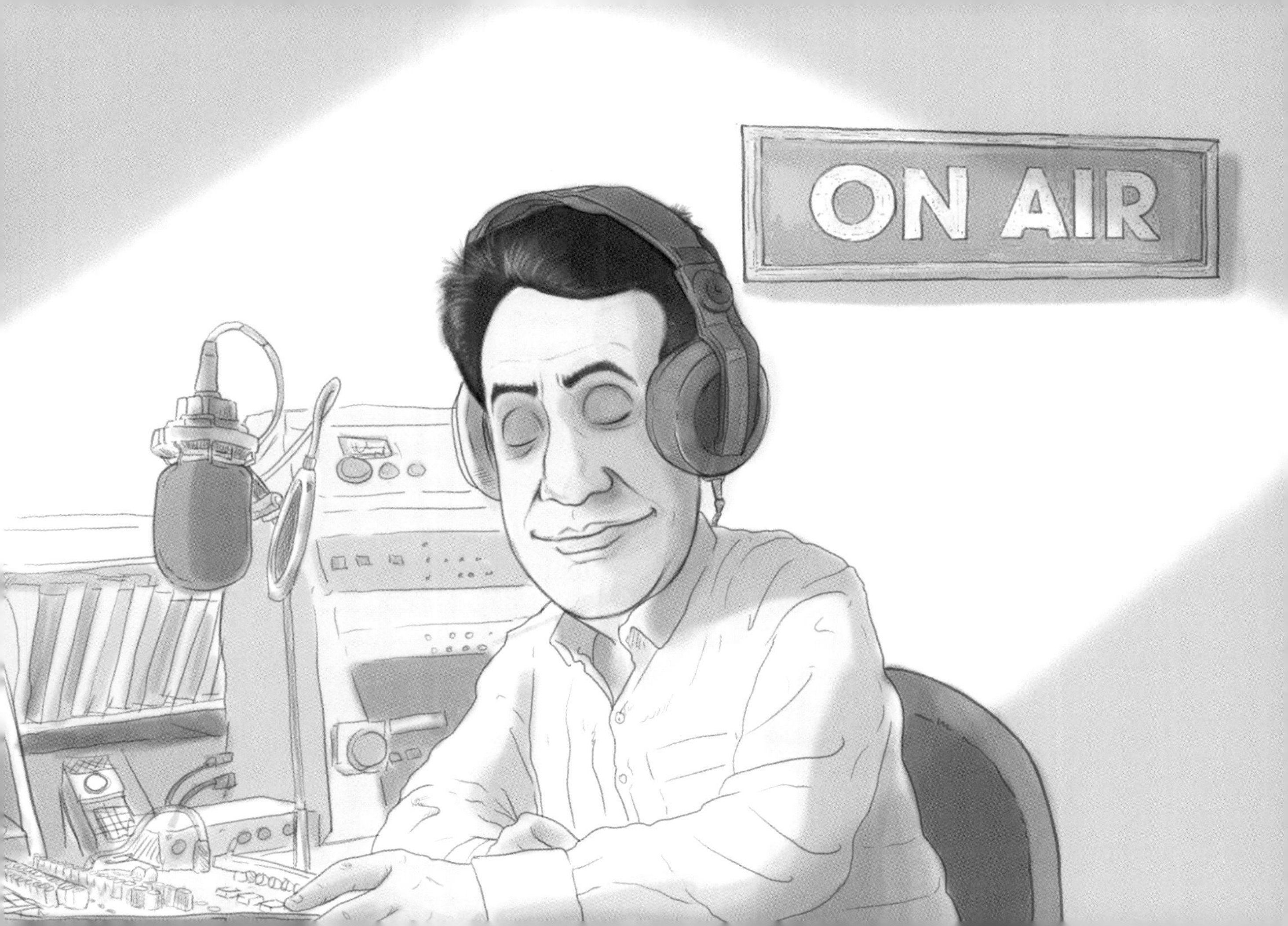
ON AIR

**24 June 2017**
Labour leader Jeremy Corbyn makes an appearance on the Pyramid Stage at Glastonbury, urging the crowd to 'build bridges, not walls'.


**TODAY ED MILIBAND...**
put on his warrior's robe (dressing gown) and used six recycled kitchen roll tubes and some tinfoil to make a sword.

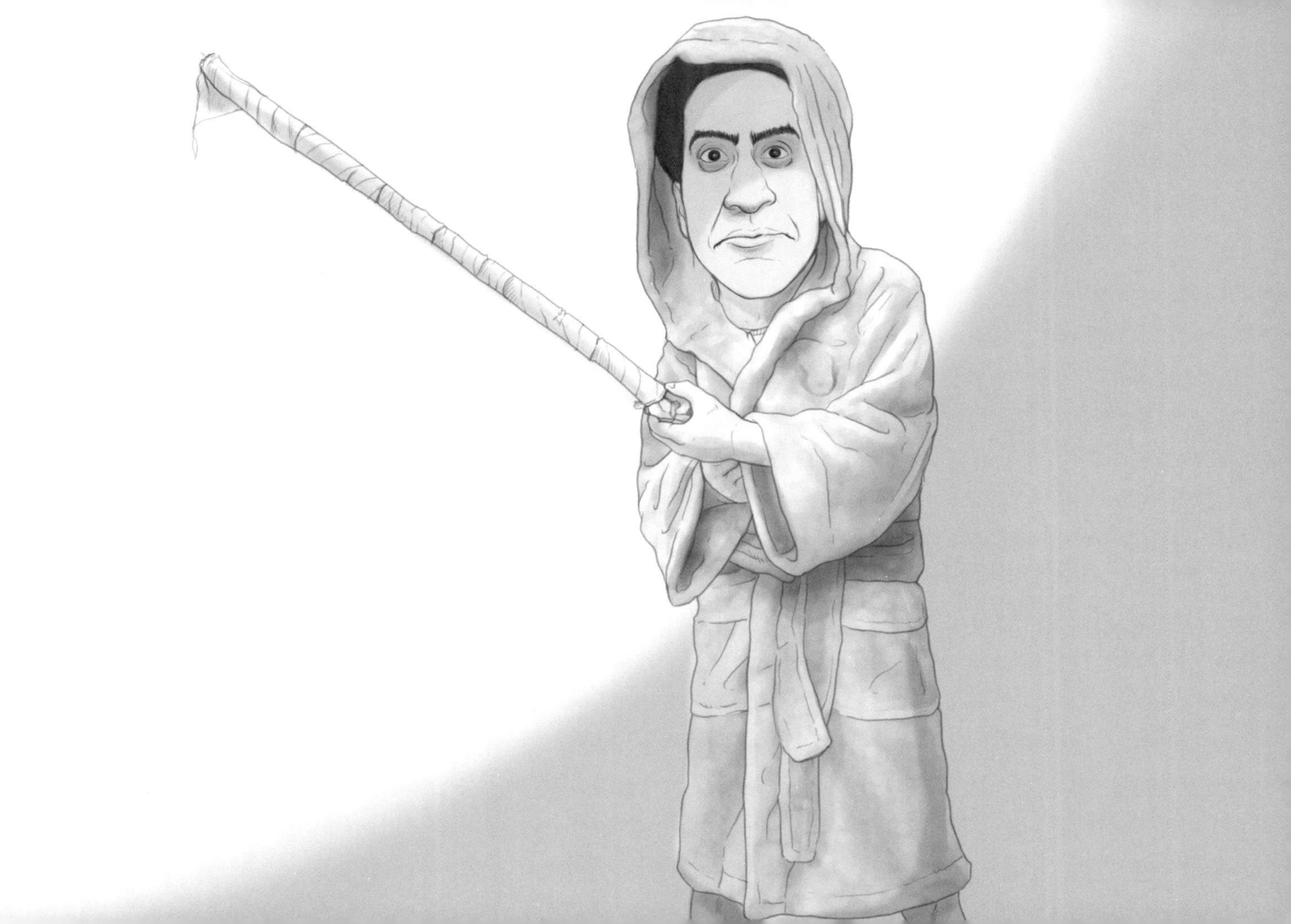

**26 June 2017**

The Conservative government agrees a £1 billion deal with Northern Ireland's Democratic Unionist Party (DUP) to secure their support. The 318 Tory MPs and 10 DUP MPs now make up over half the MPs in the House of Commons.

**TODAY ED MILIBAND...**

gave his friend Pedro a lift to King's Cross station to catch a train to Edinburgh. After miscalculating the traffic on Holloway Road and causing him to miss it, the burden of guilt proved too much. Ended up driving him the whole way, via a seven-hour sleep in a Tesco car park on the way back. Total travel time: 25.4 hours.

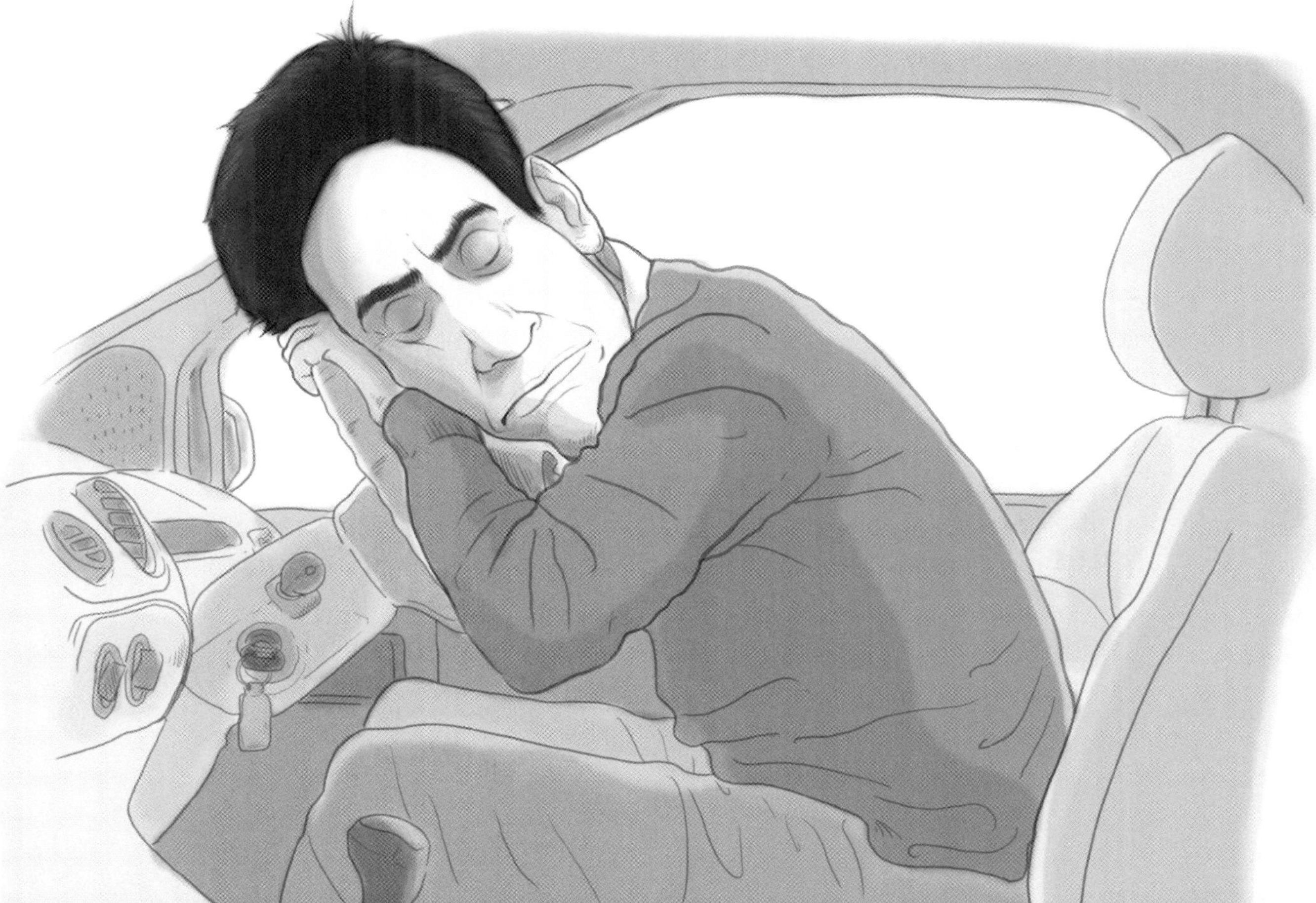

**8 December 2017**
The UK and EU publish a joint report on progress made during Phase 1 of negotiations, including the expected 'divorce bill' of between £35-39bn. This concludes Phase 1 of negotiations and both sides move on to Phase 2: trade discussions.

**TODAY ED MILIBAND…**
hit a new personal best! Made it over a week into December before watching *The Muppet Christmas Carol*. Previous record: 6 December. Previous low point: 12 August.

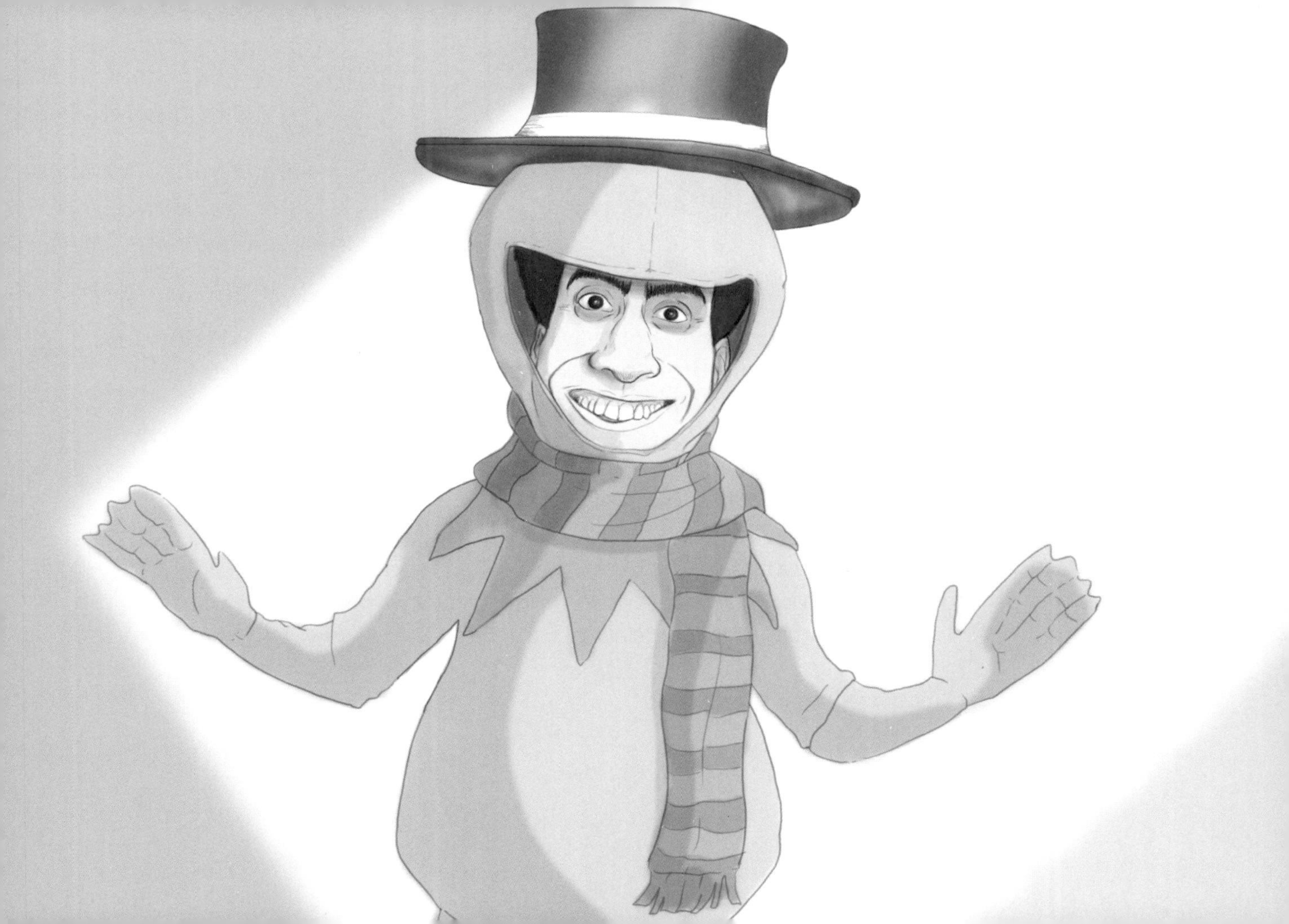

**6 July 2018**
In a UK Cabinet away-day at Chequers, Prime Minister Theresa May sets out her deal plan and key principles for Brexit. Brexiteers and Eurosceptic MPs voice concerns that it amounts to a soft Brexit.


**TODAY ED MILIBAND…**
had a day of ups and downs. Enjoyed the quarterly boys' afternoon out to Laser Quest and finished third out of five – not too shabby! – but did twist his ankle after attacking the ramp a bit too vigorously when trying to storm the blue base turret. Additional up: had pizza for tea.

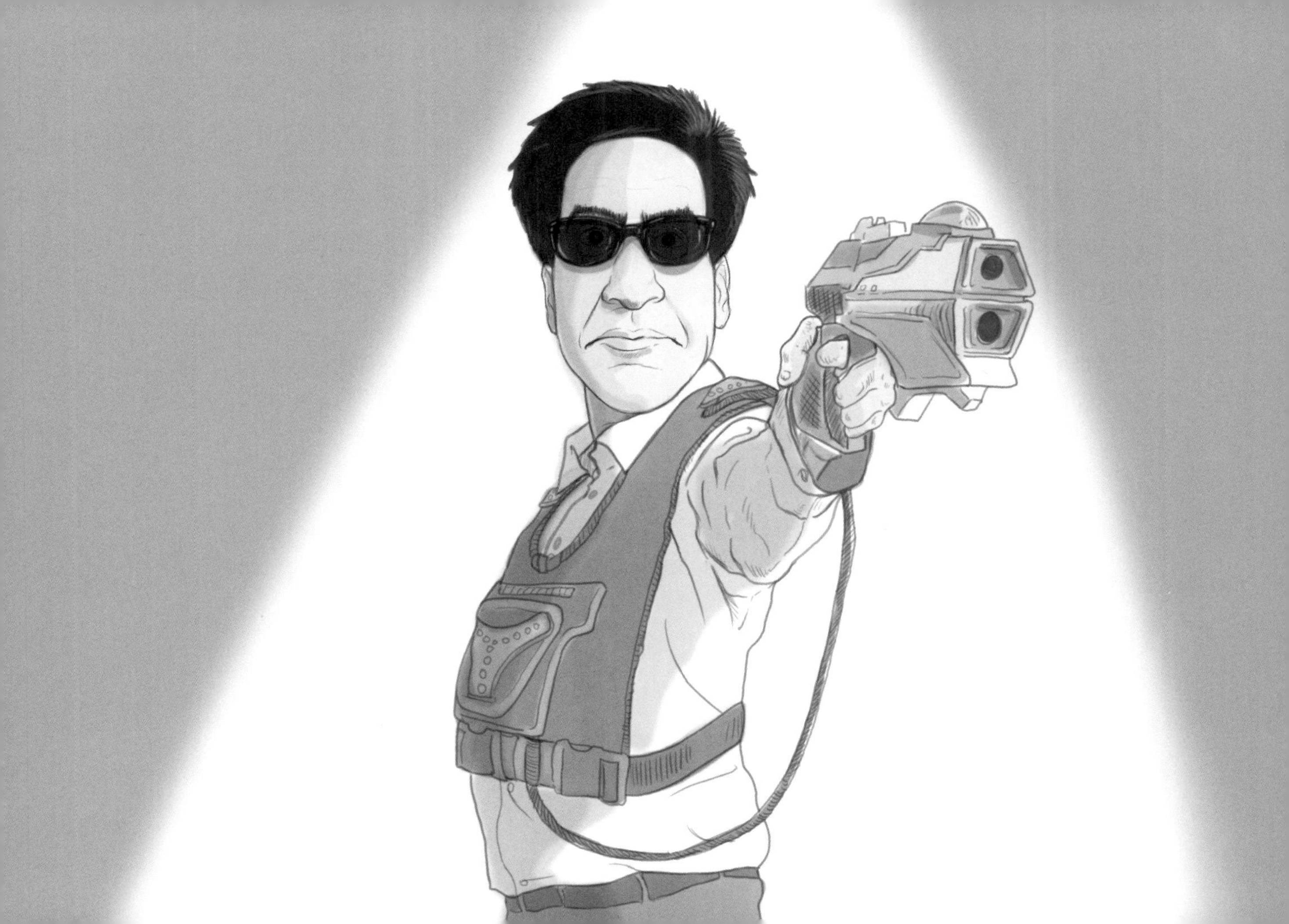

**8 July 2018**
Unhappy with the Prime Minister's Chequers plan for a 'soft' Brexit, David Davis resigns as Secretary of State for Exiting the European Union. He is replaced by Dominic Raab.

**TODAY ED MILIBAND...**
messaged David to tell him he's mastered his choux pastry recipe.
No reply, but he's a busy guy, it's cool. He'll reply later!

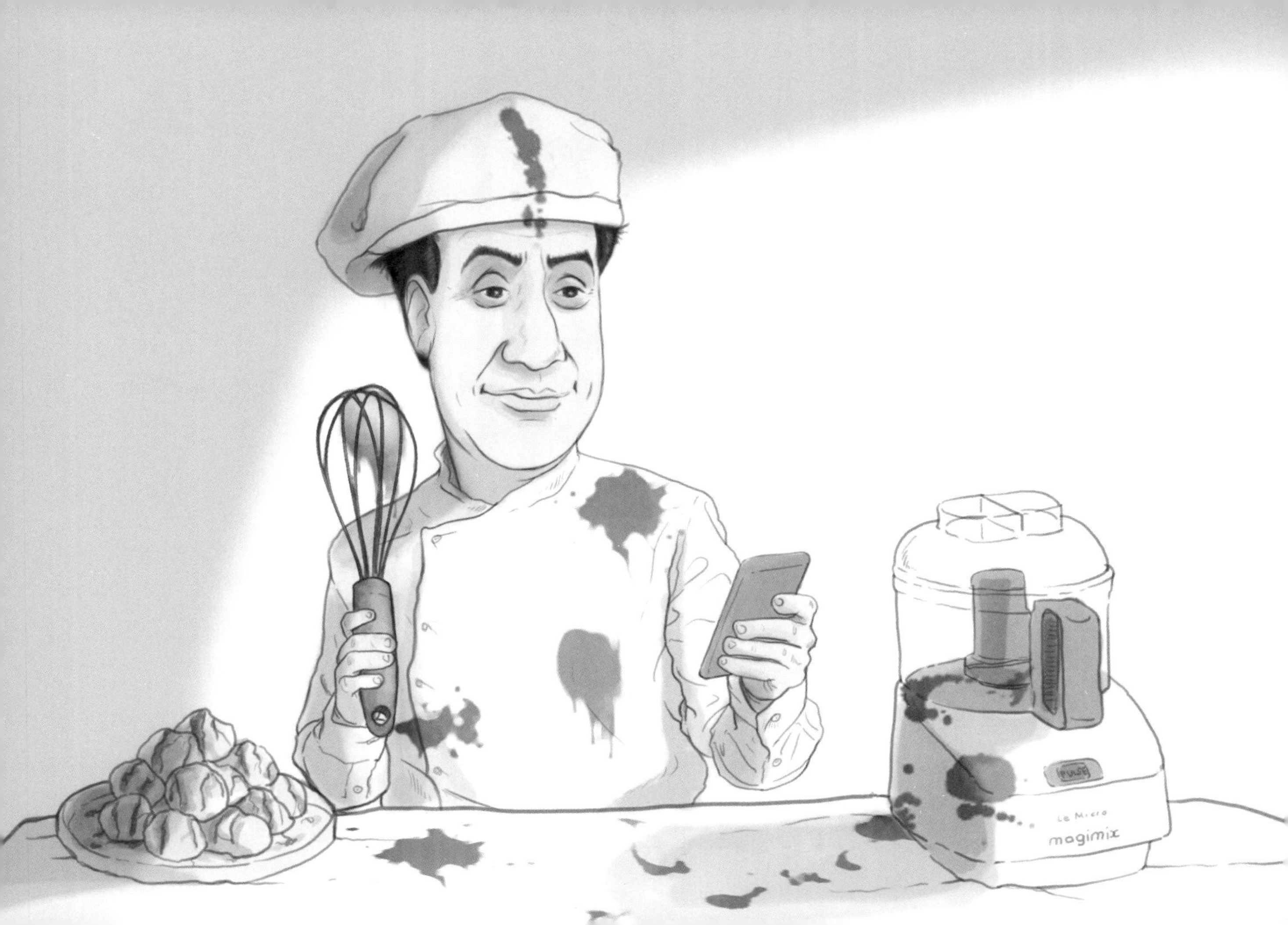
Le Micro
magimix

**9 July 2018**
Unhappy with the Prime Minister's Chequers plan for a 'soft' Brexit, Boris Johnson resigns as Foreign Secretary. He is replaced by Jeremy Hunt.


**TODAY ED MILIBAND...**
took a lavender bath to 'take the edge off' after realising David had definitely read that WhatsApp. Two blue ticks. *Last seen today at 17:08*. Still no reply.

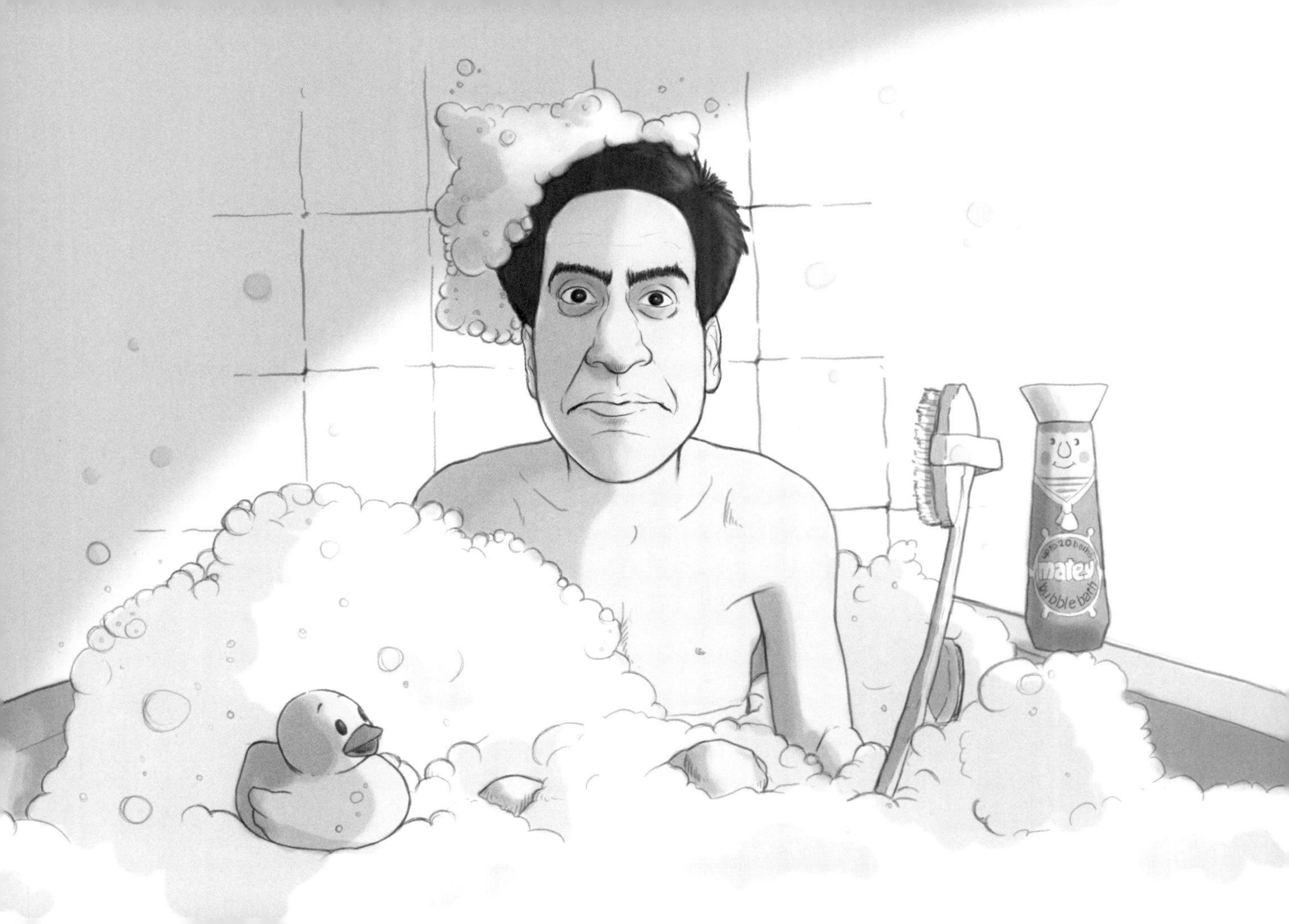
matey
bubble bath

**13 July 2018**
A giant baby blimp of US President Donald Trump flies over London as part of protests about his first visit to the UK since being elected.


**TODAY ED MILIBAND...**
took the old lady next door's Miniature Schnauzer to the vet. Turns out she'd drastically underestimated the bill so had to cover it. Didn't have the heart to ask for the £495.95 back from her.

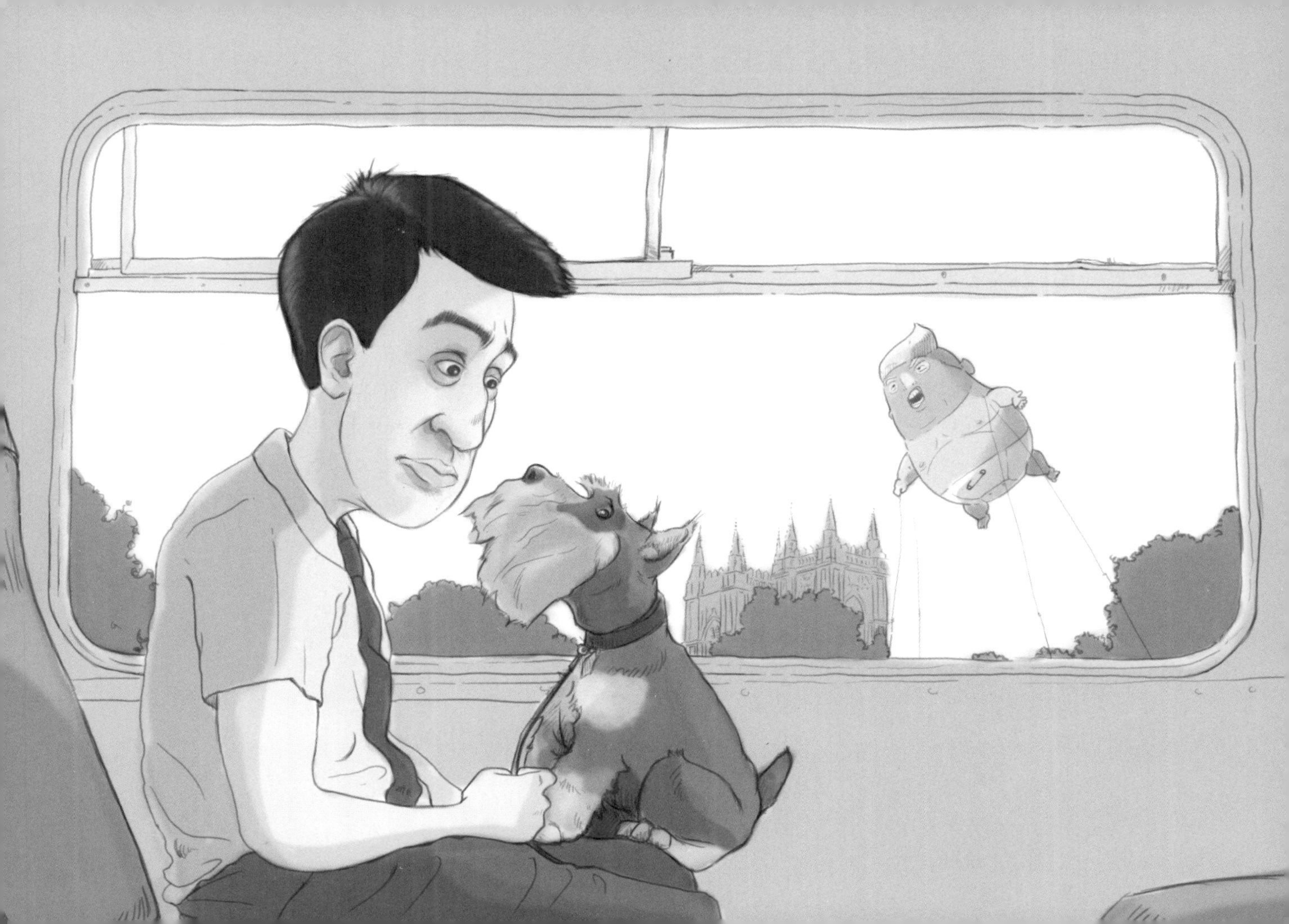

**3 October 2018**
At the Conservative Party Conference in Birmingham, Theresa May enters the stage for her speech by 'dancing' to Abba's 'Dancing Queen'.


**TODAY ED MILIBAND...**
watched three hours of YouTube tutorials on the Argentine Tango, 'just in case' *Strictly* come calling.

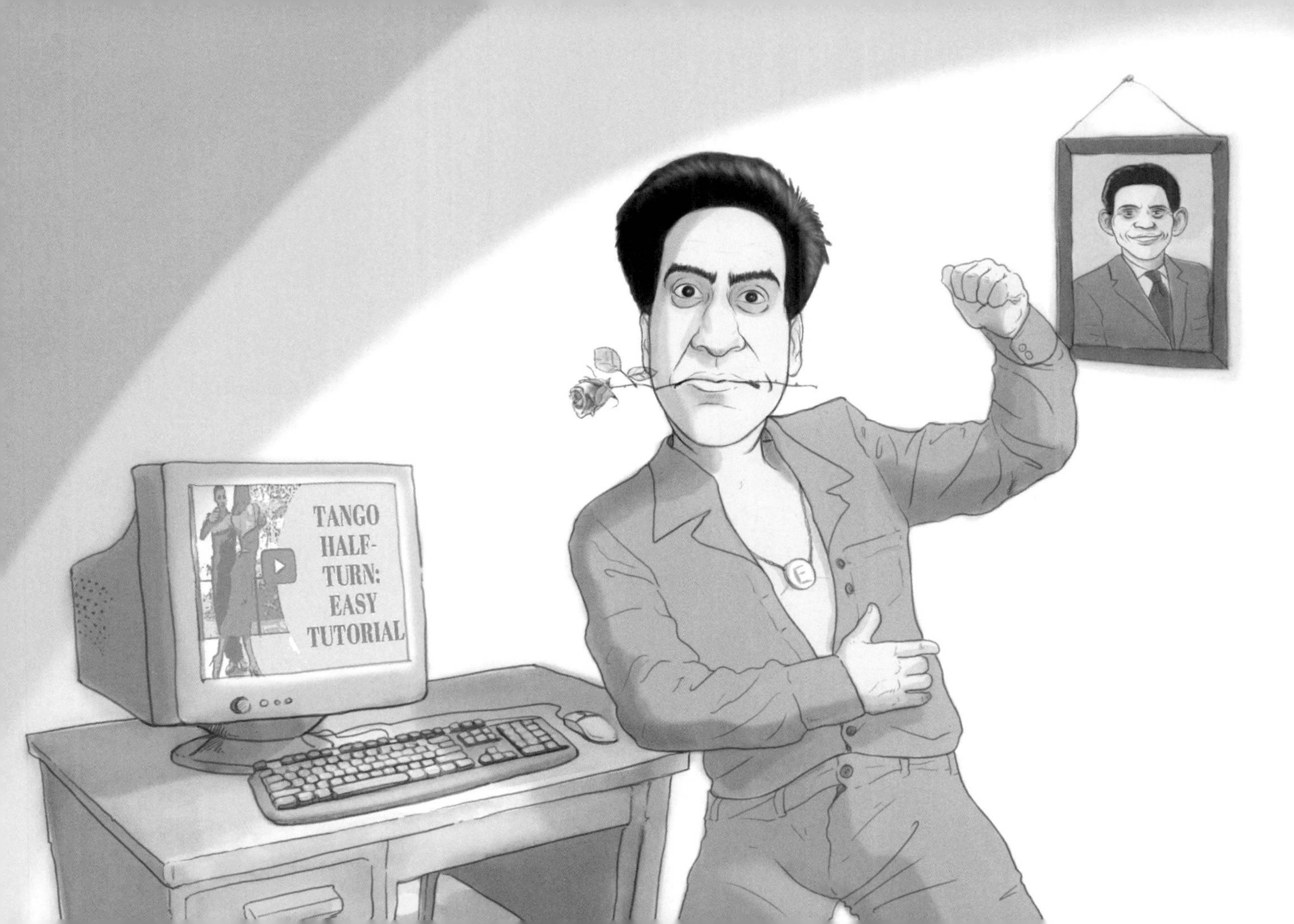
TANGO
HALF-
TURN:
EASY
TUTORIAL

**12 December 2018**
Theresa May survives of a vote of no confidence in her leadership, as tabled by Tory MPs, by 200 votes to 117.


**TODAY ED MILIBAND...**
after seven test batches – featuring increasing quantities of rum – finally nailed his eggnog recipe for the festive season. Headache risk tomorrow: high.

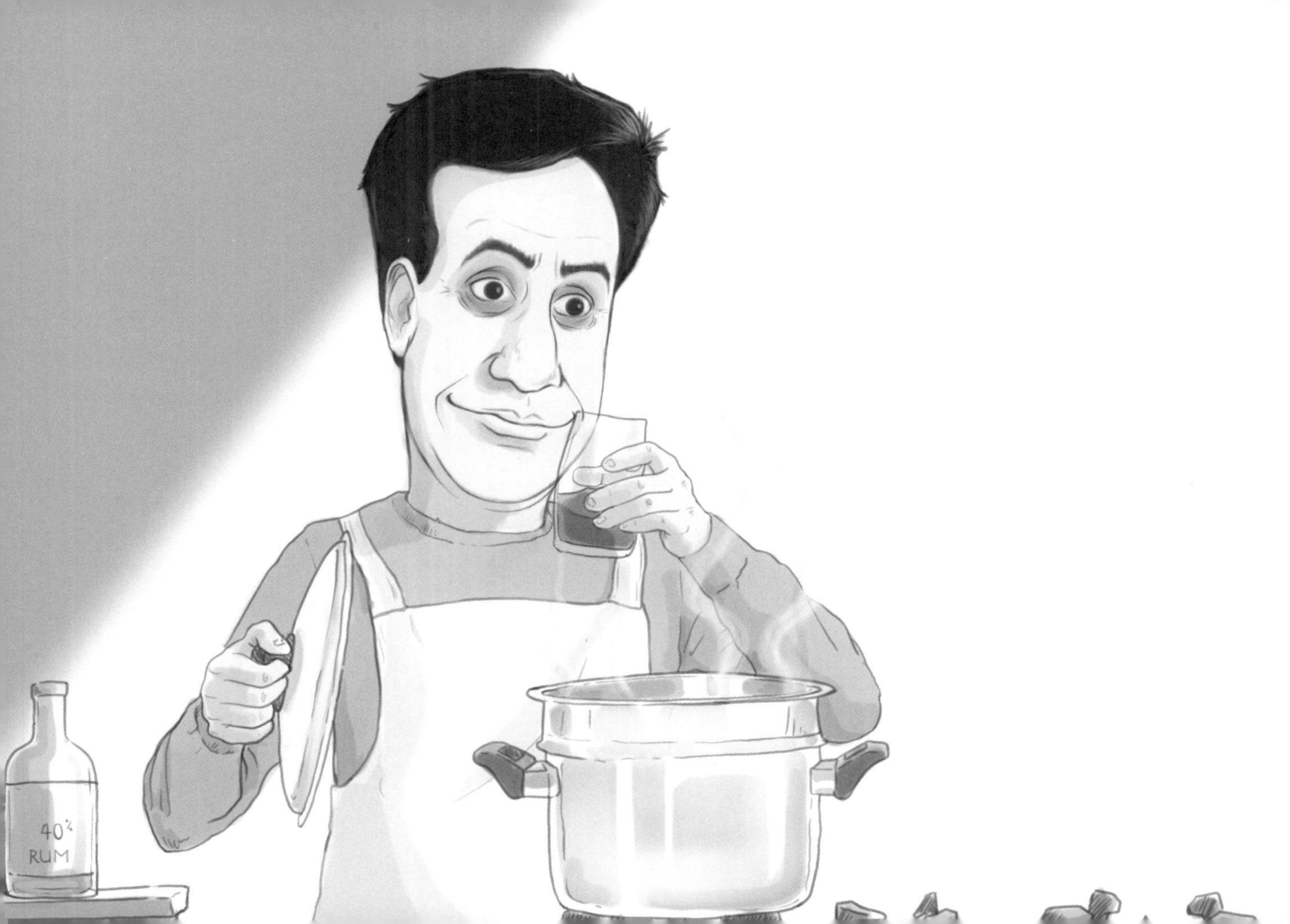
40%
RUM

**15 January 2019**
Theresa May loses a House of Commons vote on her deal to leave the EU by a margin of 230 votes (202 in favour, 432 opposed). It is the largest parliamentary defeat of any British prime minister in history.

**TODAY ED MILIBAND...**
finished his Janaury sales admin and returned a diamond-patterned sweater vest as it was just a bit too jazzy for his taste. Ordered a simple pale blue replacement.

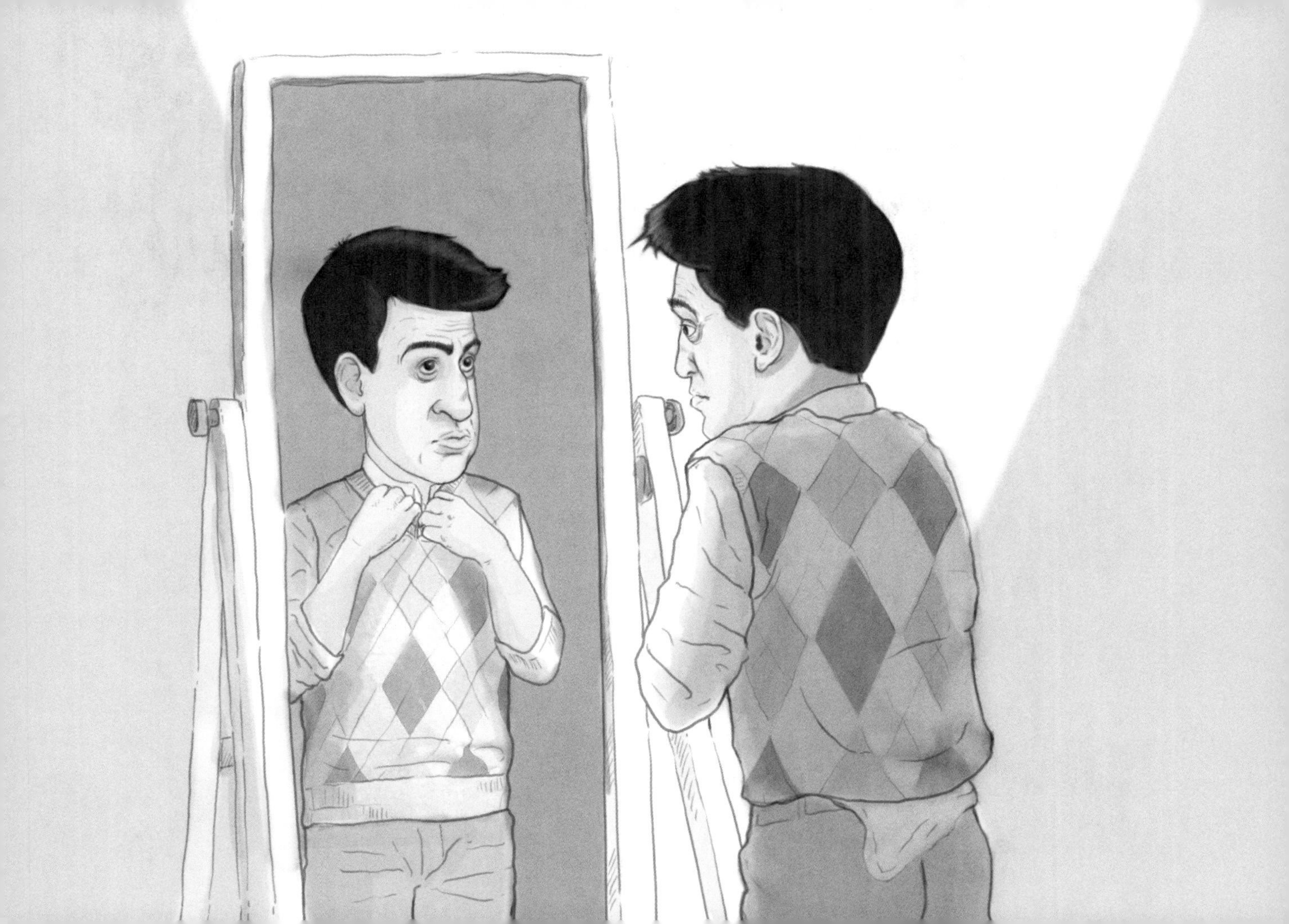

**21 January 2019**
Theresa May confirms the government will waive the £65 fee for EU nationals to apply for settled status in the UK post-Brexit.


**TODAY ED MILIBAND...**
gave up on his attempt to grow a moustache. A blatant attempt to refresh his 'Milibrand', the five days' worth of hipster 'tache proved far too itchy.

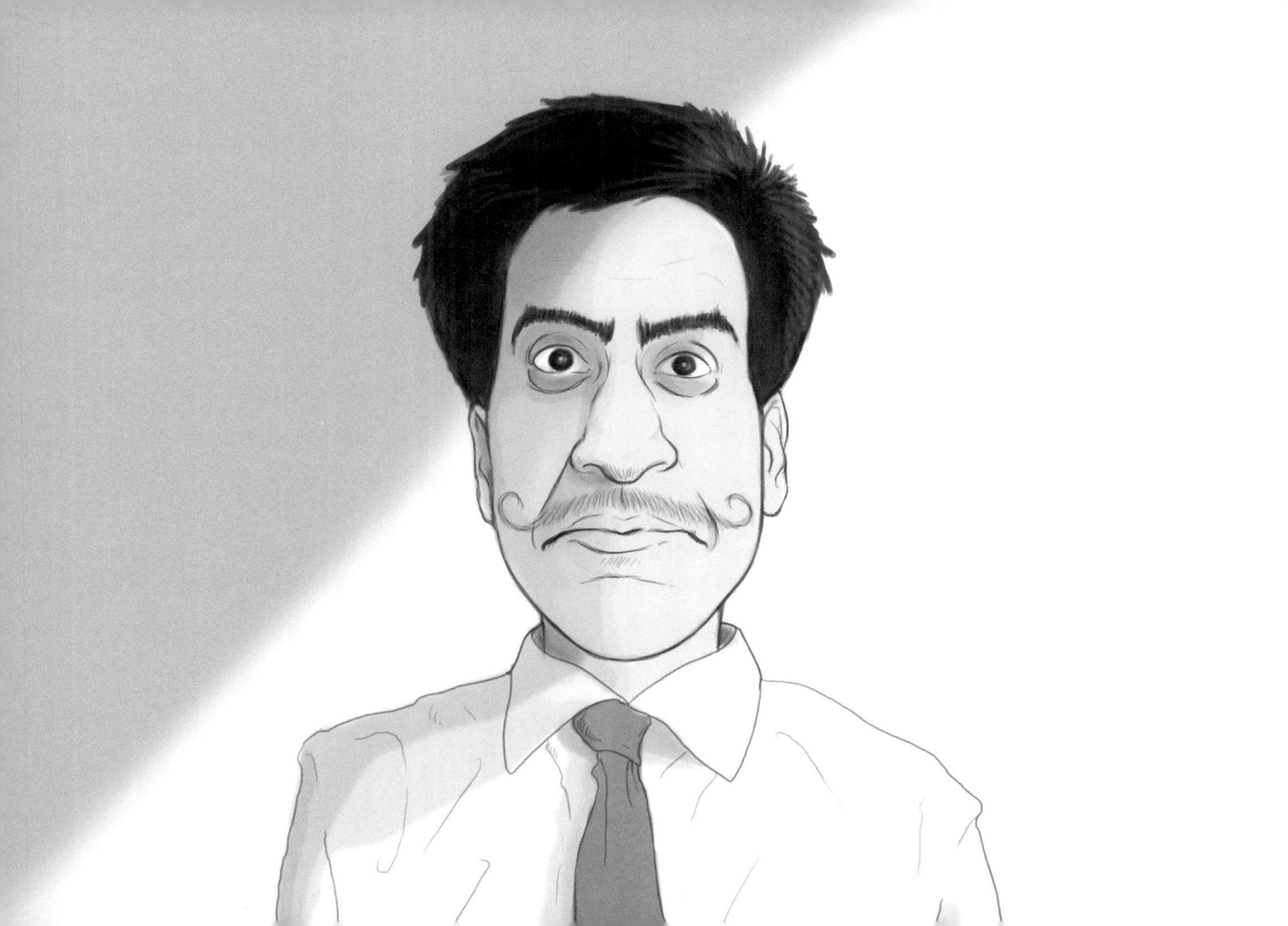

**14 February 2019**
Theresa May loses another House of Commons vote on her negotiating strategy for leaving the EU, by 303 to 258 – a majority of 45.


**TODAY ED MILIBAND...**
wrote his first joke in over four months – and what a joke it was!
'What's a cowboy's favourite brand of car?' *'An Audi, partner!'*.

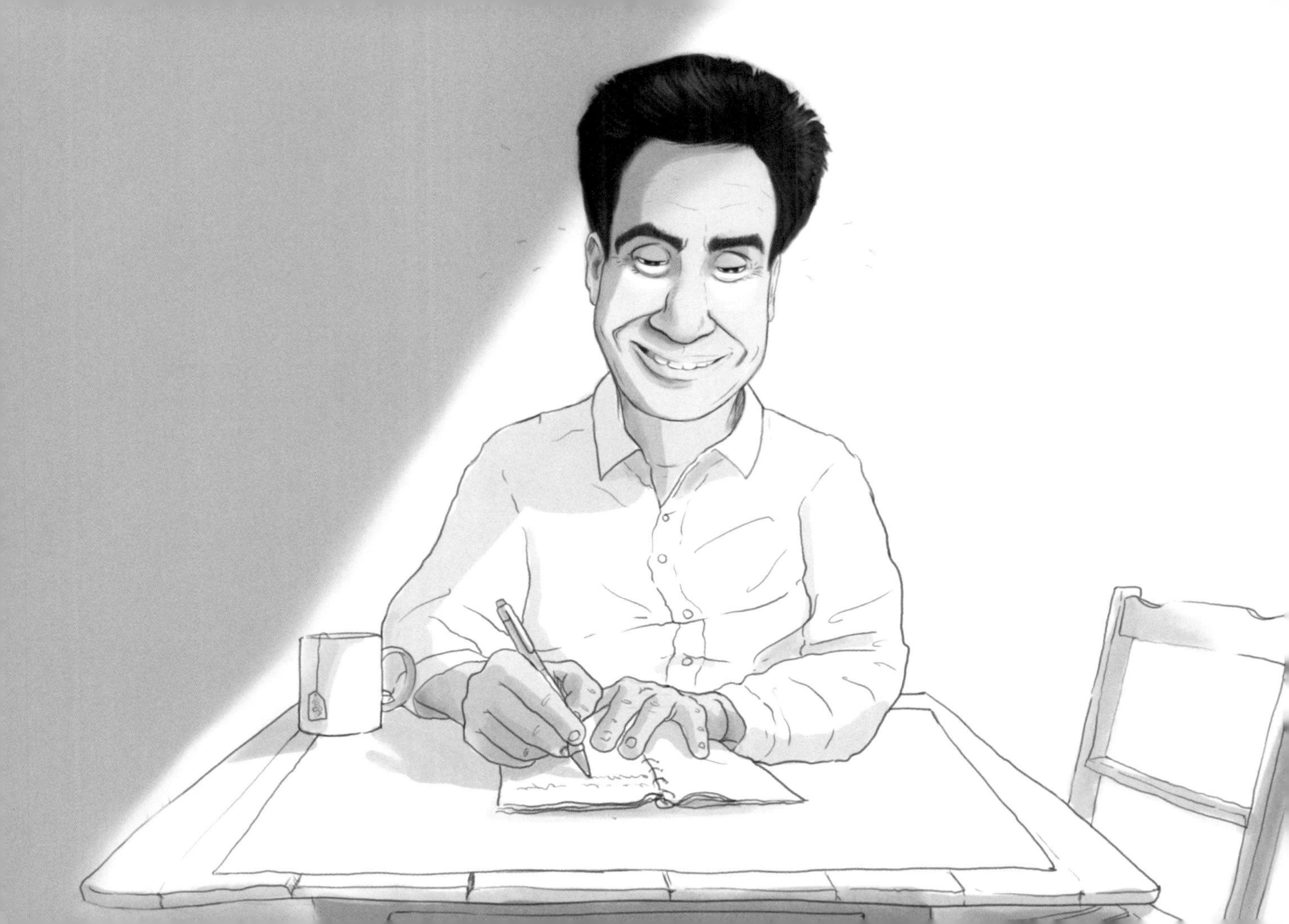

**18 February 2019**
New political party Change UK is founded by a group of Labour and Conservative MPs: Luciana Berger, Ann Coffey, Mike Gapes, Chris Leslie, Gavin Shuker, Angela Smith and Chuka Umunna.

**TODAY ED MILIBAND…**
missed a call from Chuka Umunna because he was too engrossed in the *Traffic Cops* omnibus.

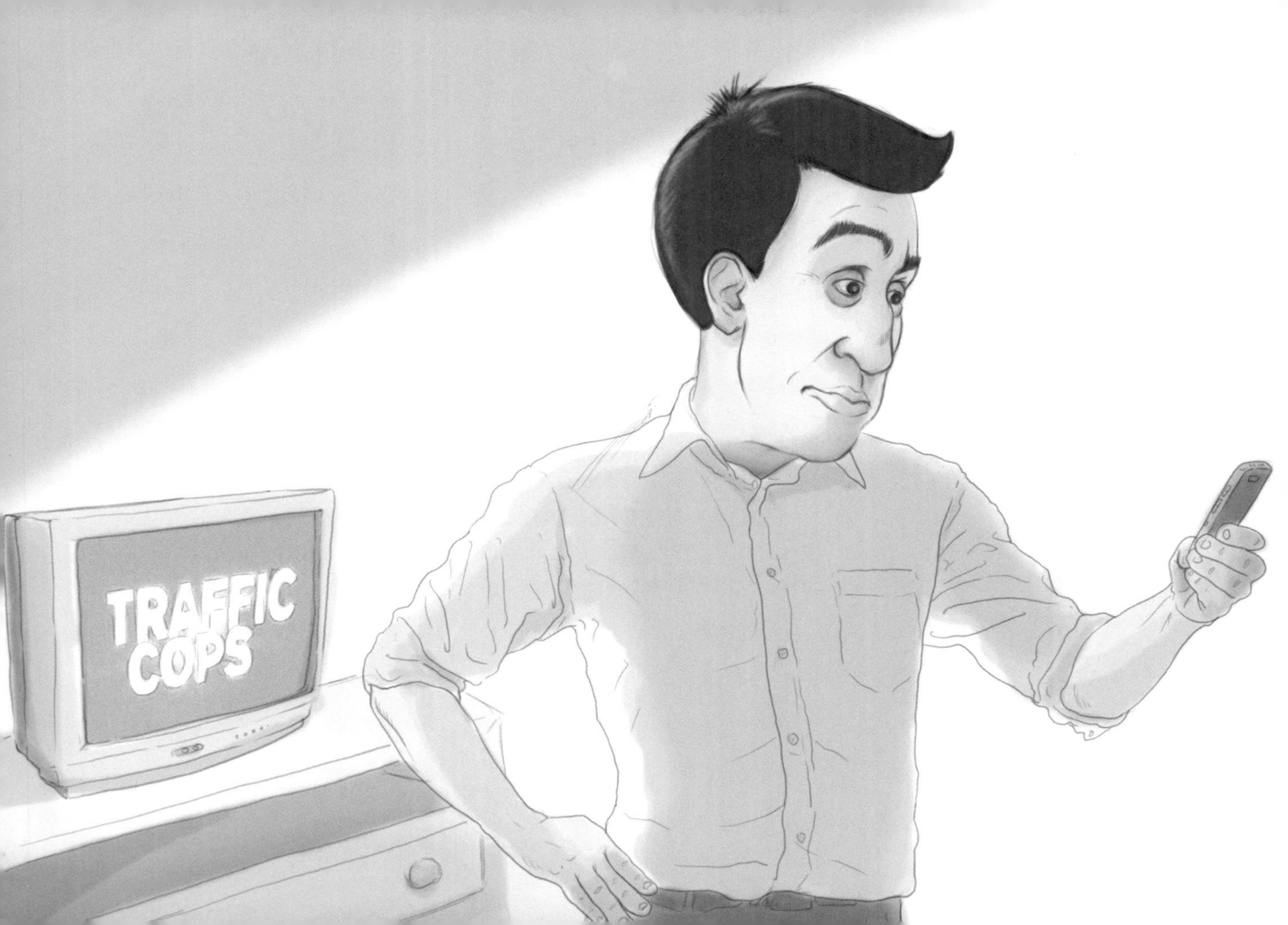
TRAFFIC
COPS

**19 February 2019**
Further MPs join Change UK, including Joan Ryan, Sarah Wollaston, Heidi Allen and Anna Soubry.


**TODAY ED MILIBAND…**
returned Chuka Umunna's missed call. Turns out he'd dialled the wrong Ed by mistake anyway. Balls.

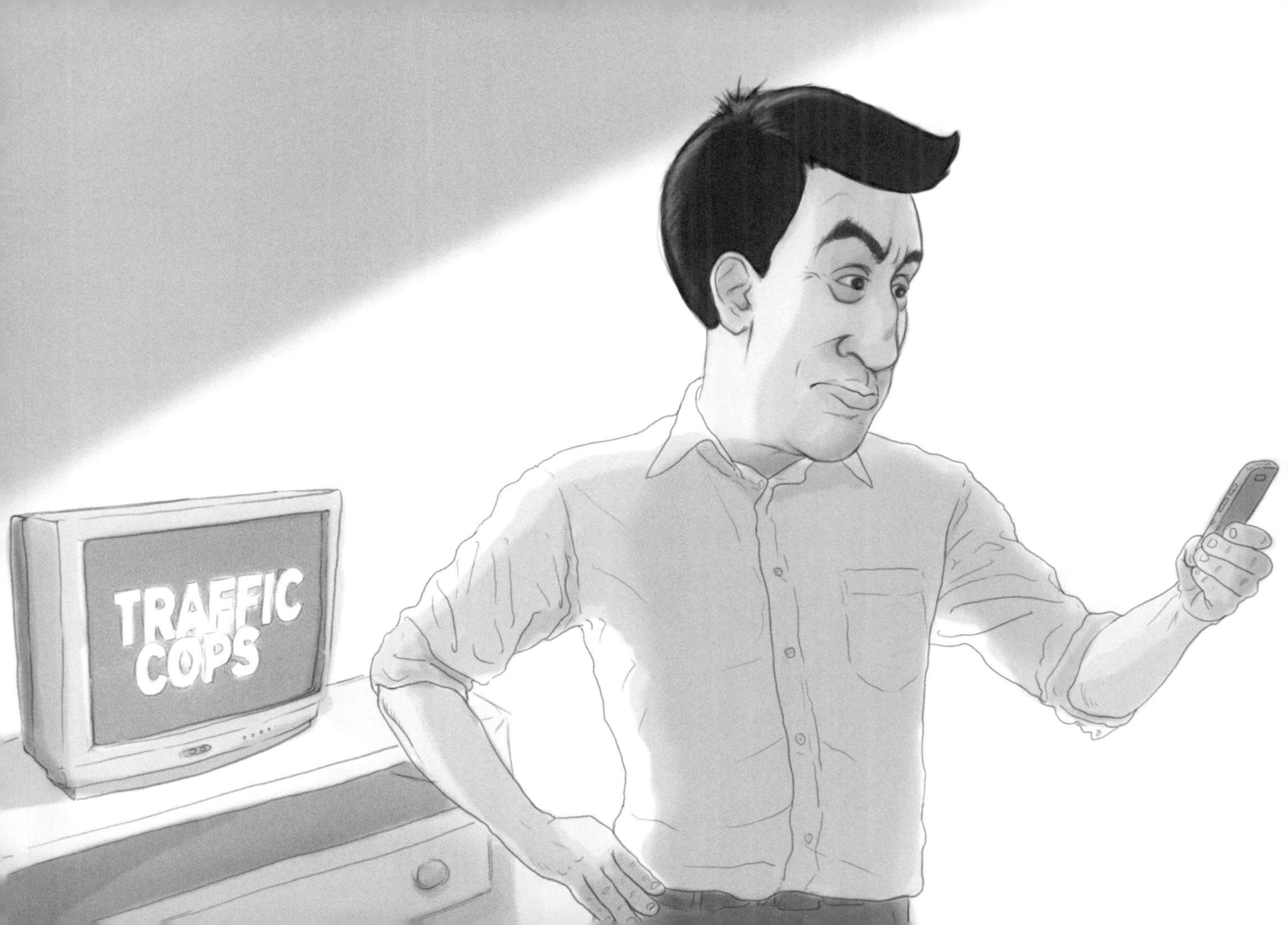
TRAFFIC
COPS

**12 March 2019**
Theresa May suffers ANOTHER defeat as MPs reject her Brexit deal for the second time, this time by a majority of 149 – including seventy-five rebel Conservatives.


**TODAY ED MILIBAND...**
got asked for a selfie by a bloke in a local café. Was happy to oblige, despite the man calling him 'David' four times.

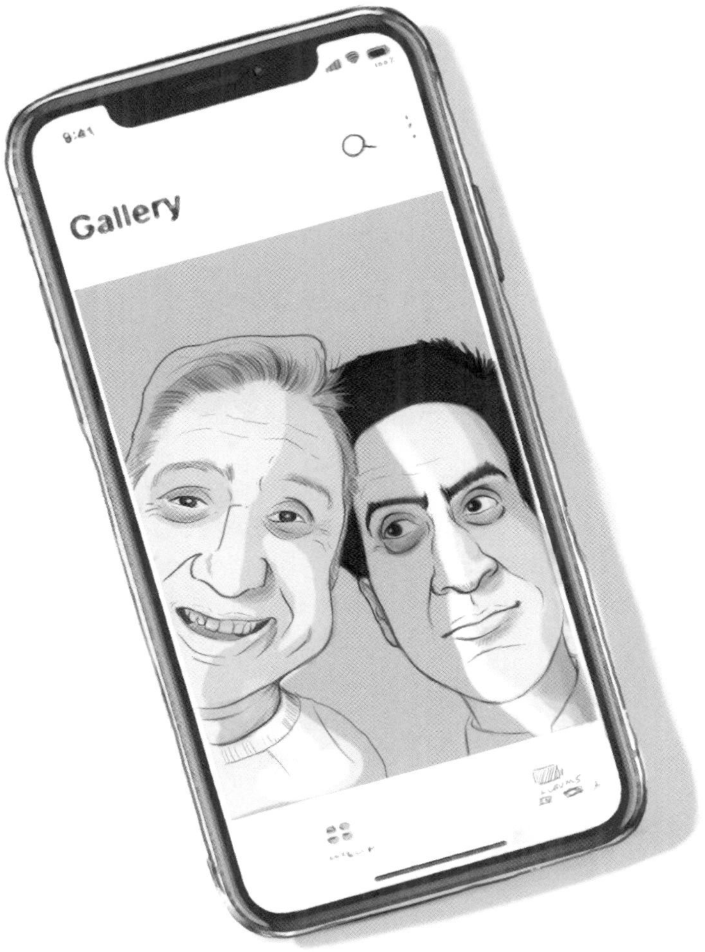
9:41
Gallery

**21 March 2019**
Theresa May goes to Brussels to try and secure an extension to the Article 50 process. The EU agrees to a delay until 22 May if she can gain approval for her exit deal by the end of March. If she can't, then the UK must leave on 12 April.


**TODAY ED MILIBAND...**
found an injured bee in the garden. Took him in, fed him some sugar water and made a makeshift bed in the spare room so he could rest up. Named him Virgil, after his favourite Tracy brother from *Thunderbirds*.

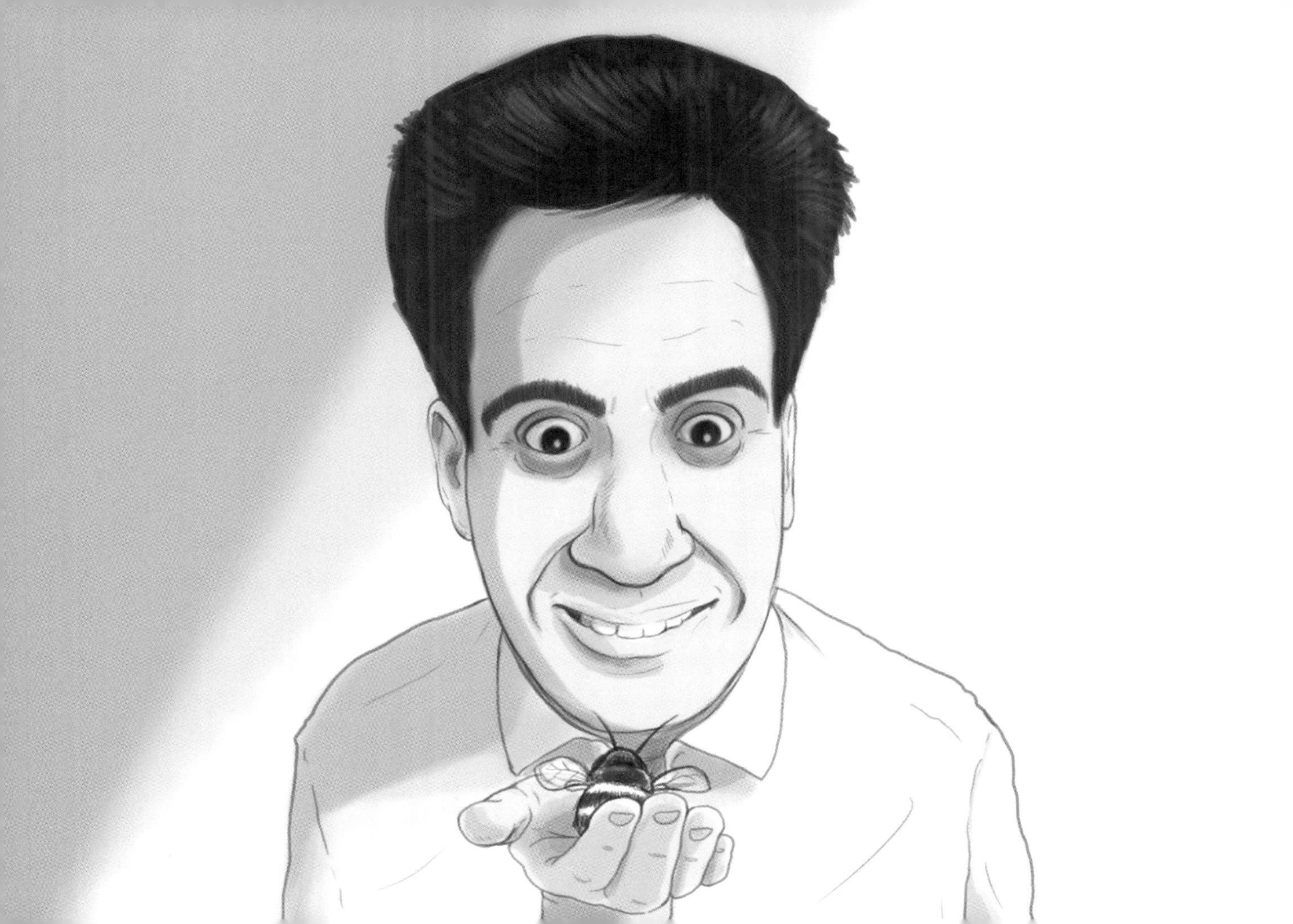

**23 March 2019**
The People's Vote march takes place in London, with official figures putting the number of people taking part at over one million.


**TODAY ED MILIBAND...**
tried again to refresh his 'Milibrand'. Experimented with putting his hair in a man bun. Didn't work, but forgot all about it and accidentally wore it to Tesco Express.

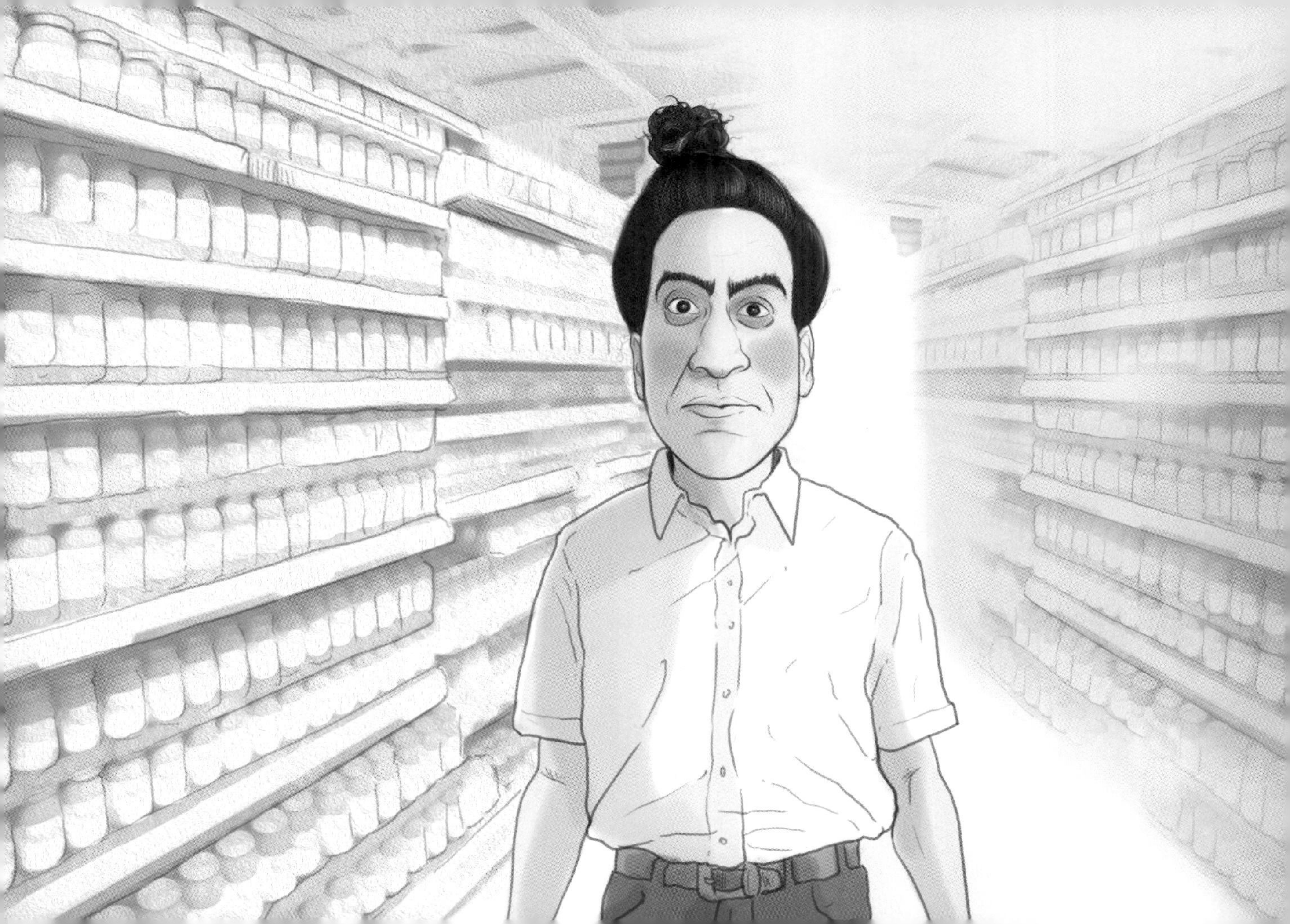

**29 March 2019**
On the day that the UK was originally meant to leave the EU, Theresa May suffers
ANOTHER defeat as MPs reject her Brexit deal for the third time, this time by a
majority of fifty-eight.


**TODAY ED MILIBAND...**
said a tearful goodbye to Virgil the bee, who is now over triple the average
weight for a bee having progressed to a regular diet of smoked salmon and
pineapple chunks. Both parties agreed it was time for him to move on. However,
Ed has made it clear he's welcome back to visit any time, and has also set up
a trust fund in Virgil's name.

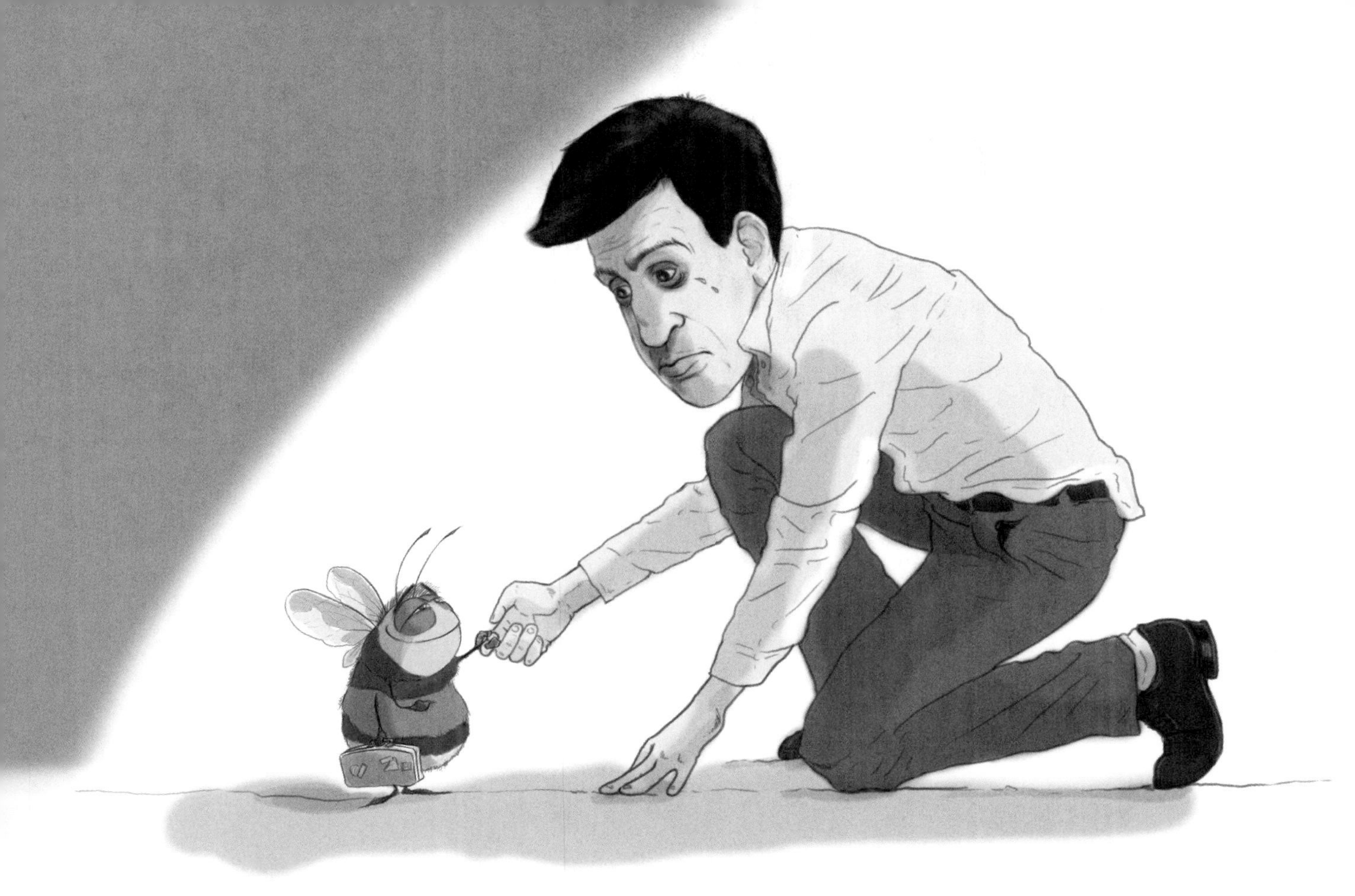

**12 April 2019**
Nigel Farage launches his new political party, the Brexit Party, in Coventry.


**TODAY ED MILIBAND...**
confirmed the plans for his annual Easter Sunday jamboree, sending a very meme-heavy email invite to every household on his street. He even invited the rude family at number 28, because everyone deserves a chance to be nice for a change.

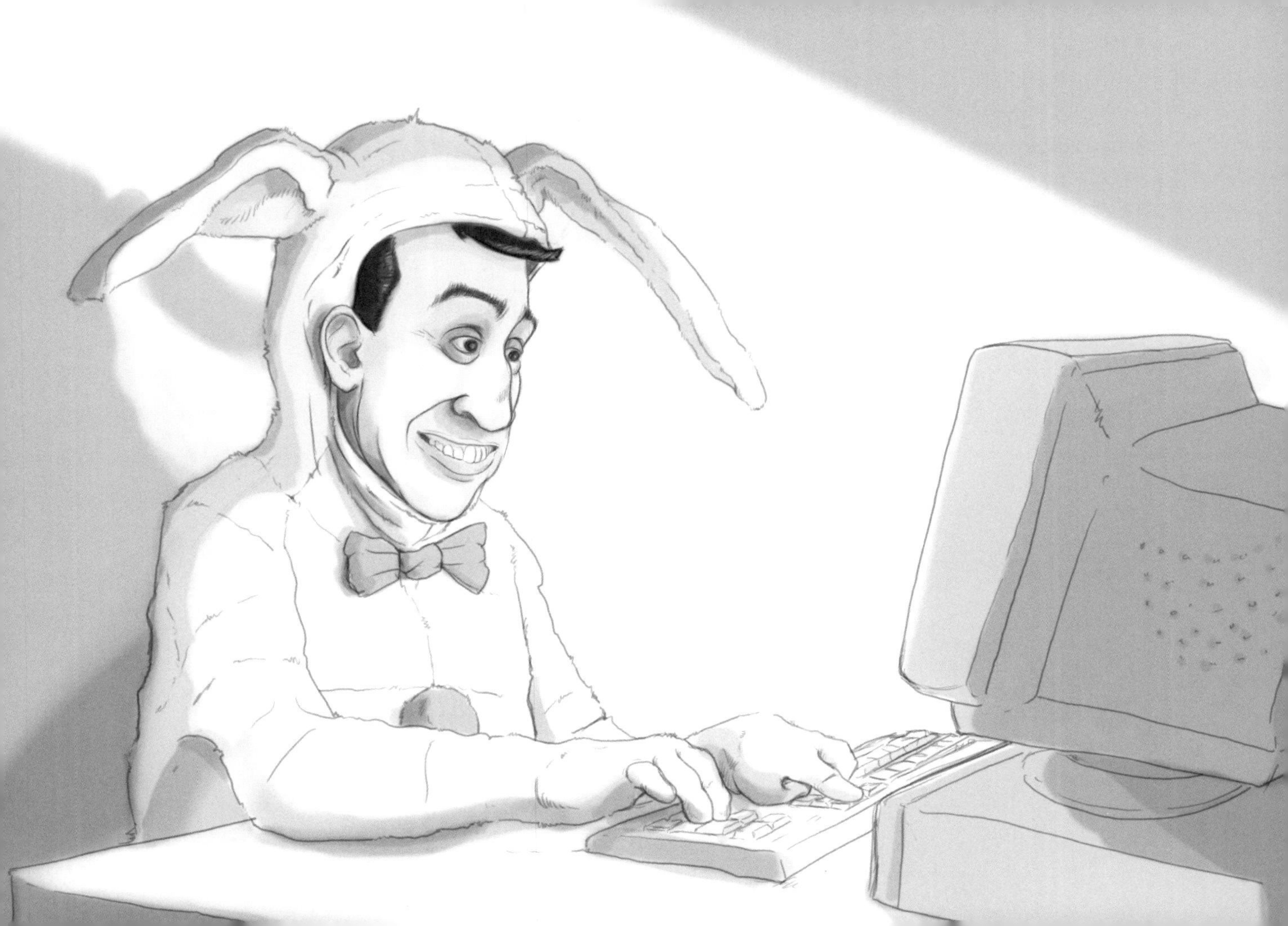

**16 May 2019**
Publisher HarperCollins confirms they will release David Cameron's
memoir, *For the Record*, on 19 September 2019.


**TODAY ED MILIBAND...**
put up two new shelves to proudly display his first edition Jilly Cooper novels.

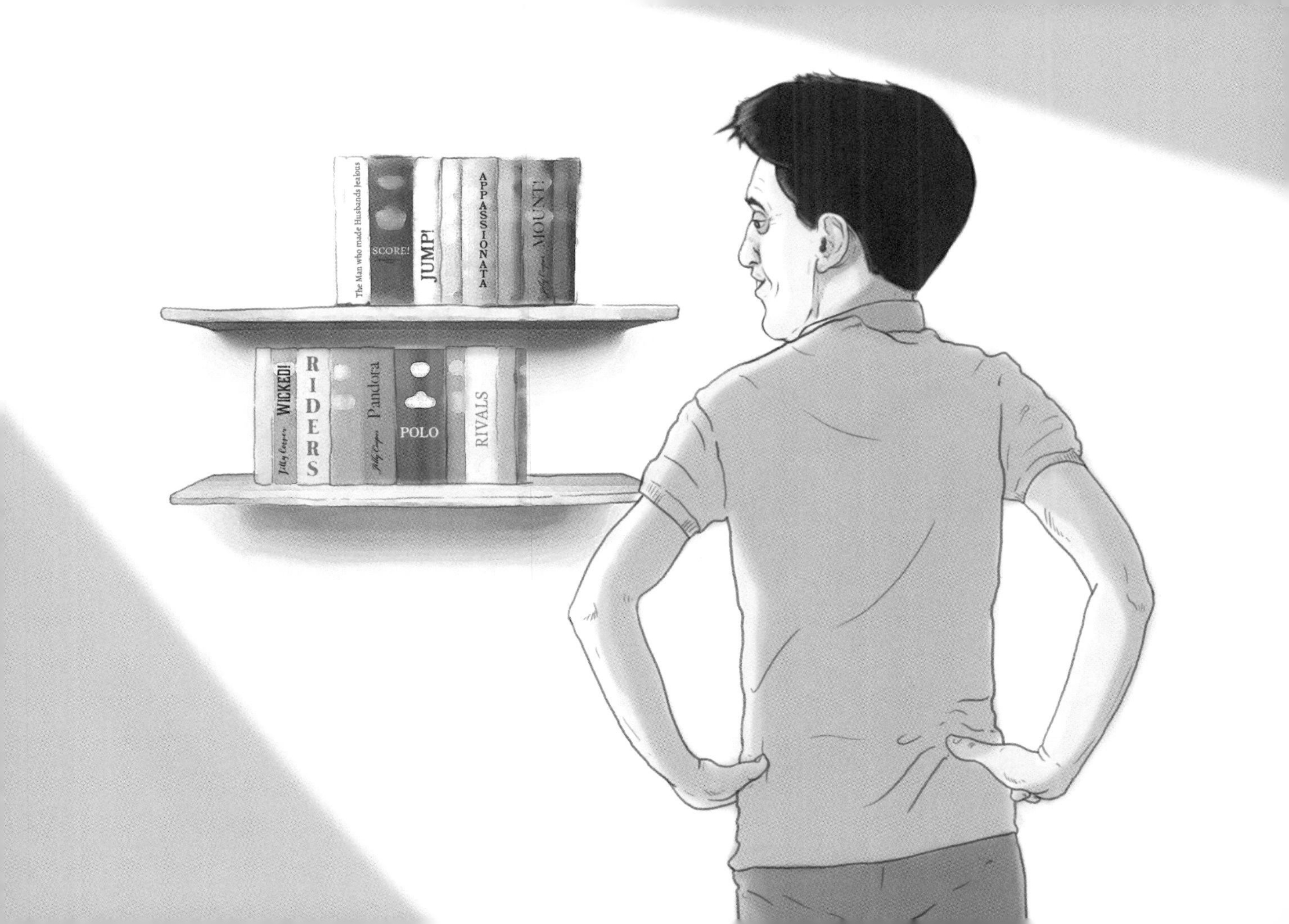
The Man who made Husbands Jealous
SCORE!
JUMP!
APPASSIONATA
MOUNT!
Jilly Cooper
WICKED!
Jilly Cooper
RIDERS
Pandora
Jilly Cooper
POLO
RIVALS

**20 May 2019**
Nigel Farage is doused in milkshake whilst out campaigning in Newcastle.


**TODAY ED MILIBAND…**
overslept after staying up late (lights out: 11.56 p.m.) watching the *Jurassic Park* Blu-ray bonus features and eating half a kilogram of Edam. Some *very* strange dreams that night.

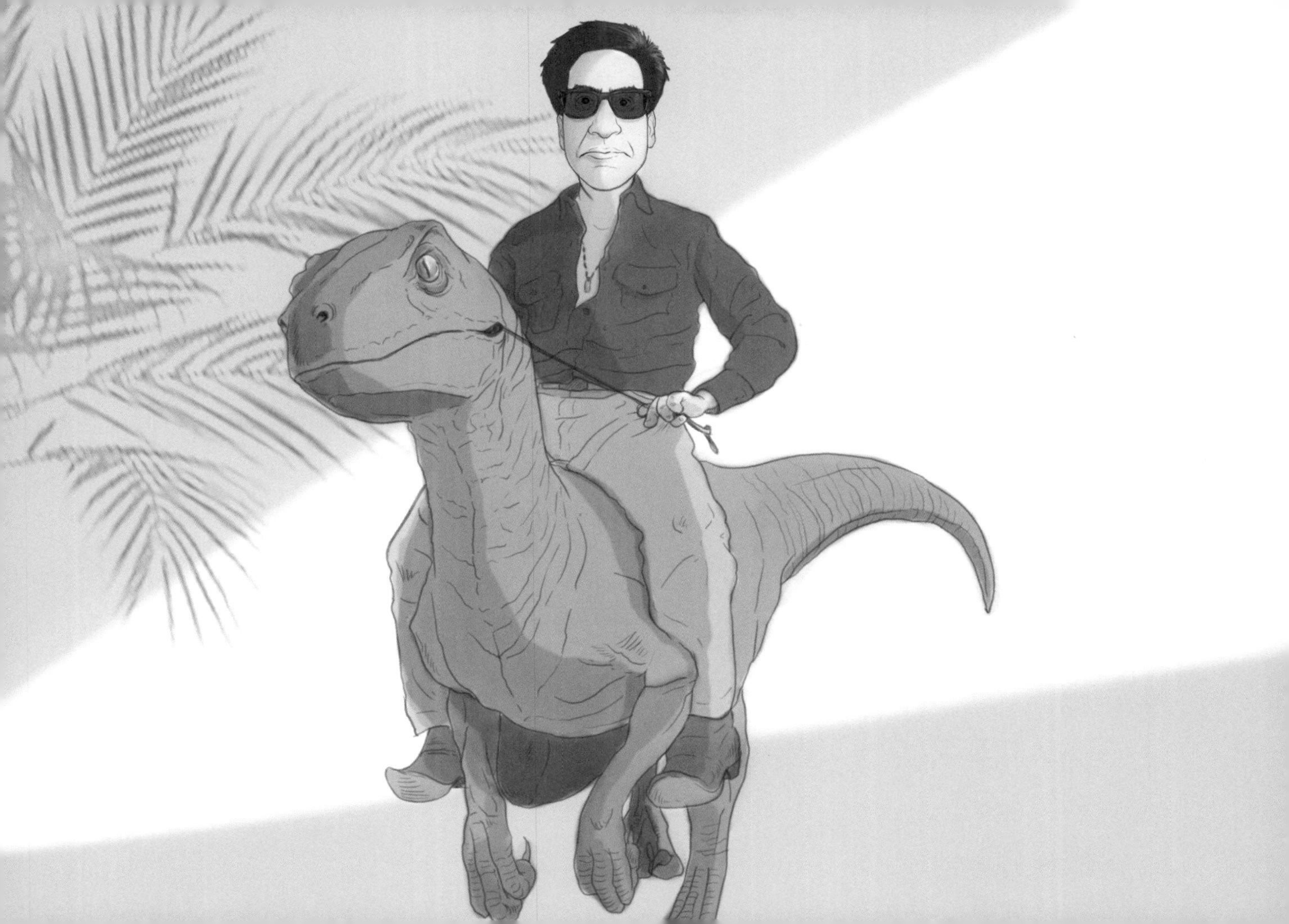

**23 May 2019**
The UK takes part in the EU parliamentary elections. The Brexit Party wins the most votes (30.5%), with the pro-Remain Liberal Democrats also making significant gains and finishing second (19.6%). Labour and the Conservatives both suffer huge losses.

**TODAY ED MILIBAND...**
voted in the morning, and then decided to treat himself to an afternoon of Scalextric, with the living room becoming an incredibly complex and high-risk circuit. In unprecedented scenes, the MiliMobile beat David Car-meron in every single race.

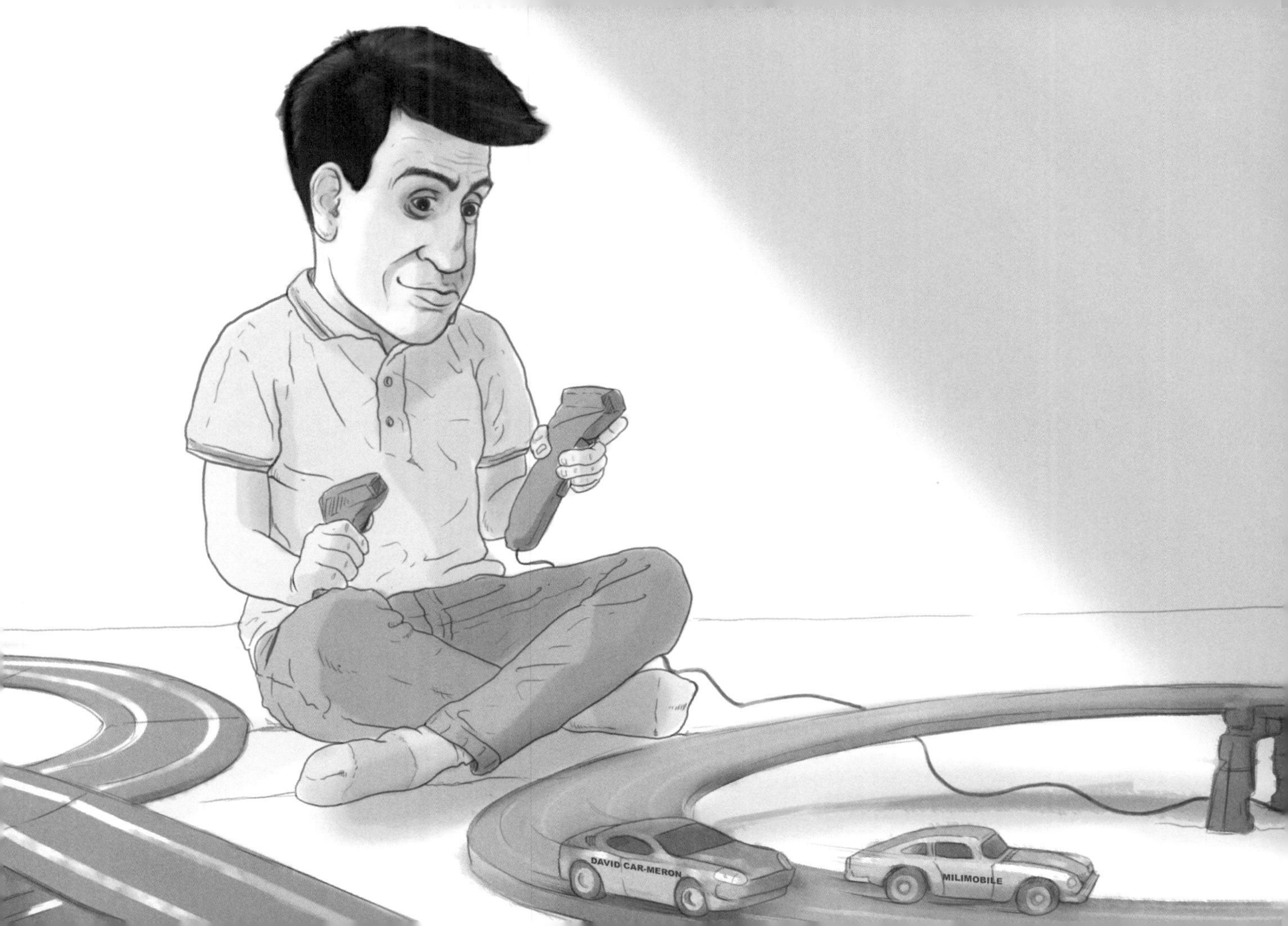
DAVID CAR-MERON
MILIMOBILE

**24 May 2019**
Theresa May confirms she will step down as prime minister on 7 June 2019, but will remain as caretaker until her successor is chosen by Conservative members.


**TODAY ED MILIBAND...**
decided to get ripped for summer. Eight press-ups, thirteen sit-ups and four grilled chicken breasts later, he ponders his next career move. Professional wrestler?

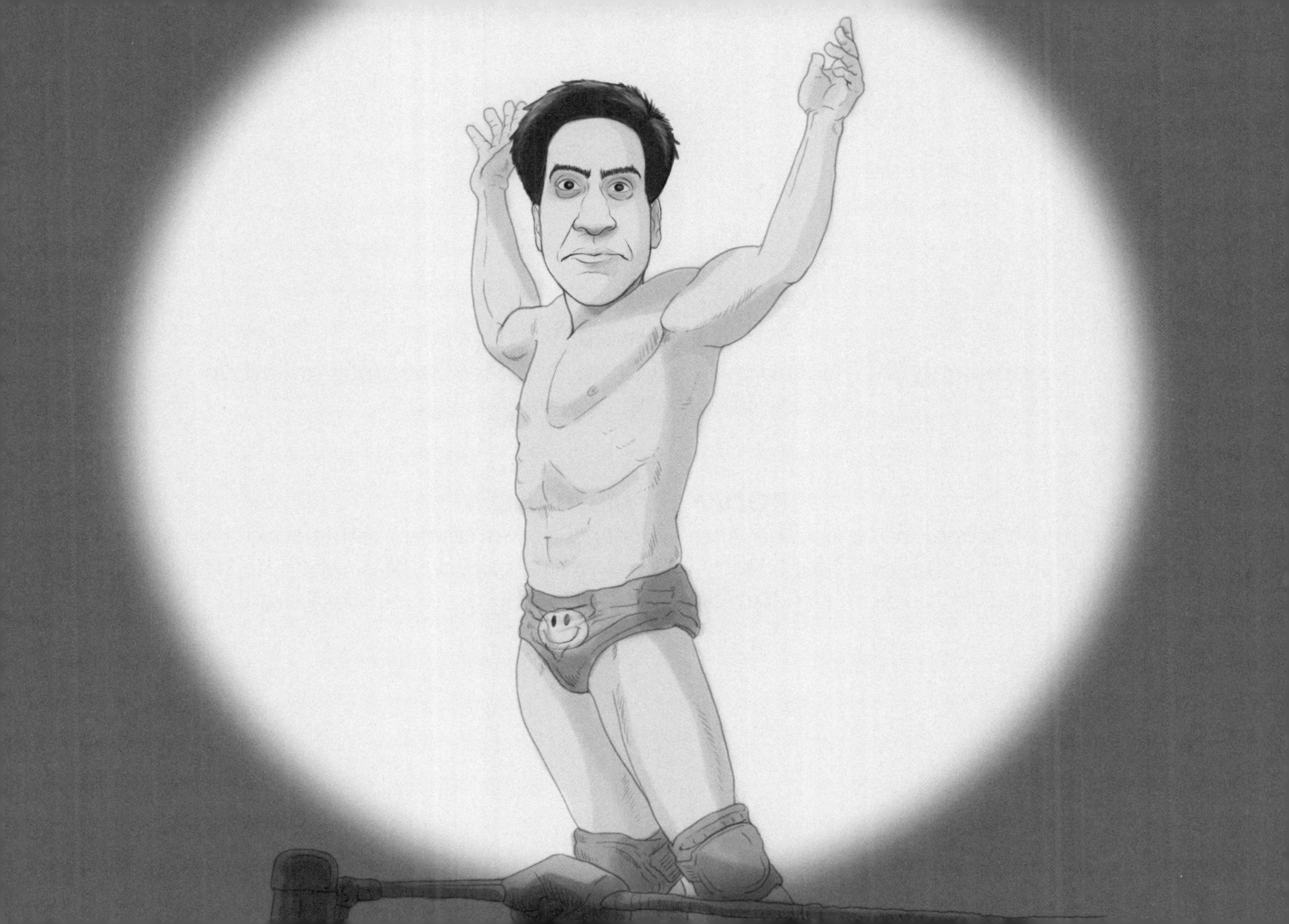

**9 June 2019**
Appearing on *The Andrew Marr Show*, Michael Gove was grilled on
his use of cocaine twenty years ago.


**TODAY ED MILIBAND...**
watched Michael Gove on *The Andrew Marr Show* and then reminisced about the
craziest night of his own life, twenty years ago in a pub in Soho, when he drank four
pints of medium strength lager and two single measures of brandy.

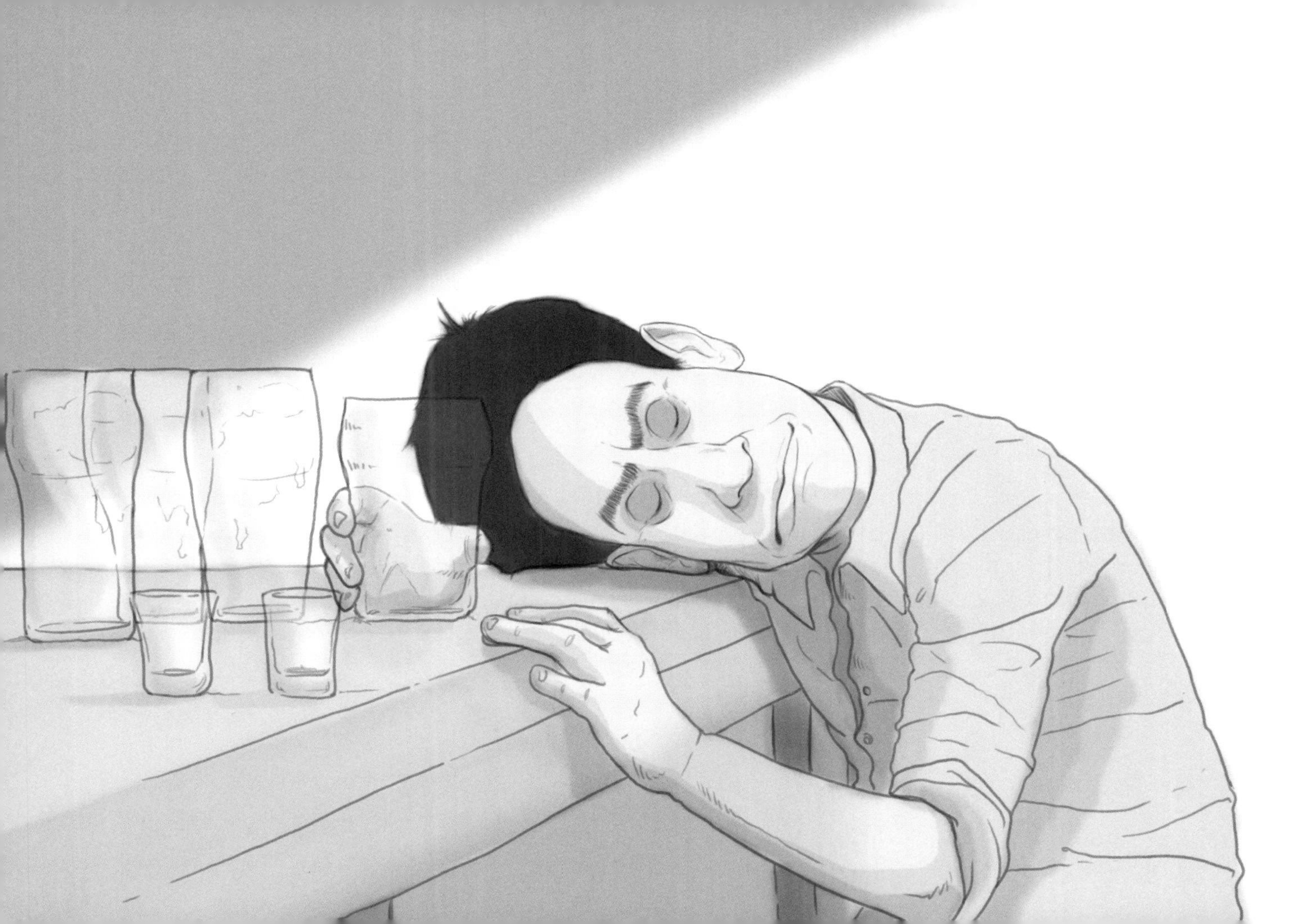

**10 June 2019**

The ten candidates to replace Theresa May as Conservative leader are confirmed: Rory Stewart, Esther McVey, Boris Johnson, Jeremy Hunt, Matt Hancock, Dominic Raab, Andrea Leadsom, Michael Gove, Sajid Javid and Mark Harper.

**TODAY ED MILIBAND...**

completed the list of his top ten favourite soft drinks of all time. In no particular order, they are: still water, sparkling water, water with slices of cucumber in, Ribena, Vimto, decaf latte, Capri-Sun (Orange), decaf Yorkshire Tea, cranberry juice and – guilty pleasure! – the weird salty liquid that pickled gherkins come in.

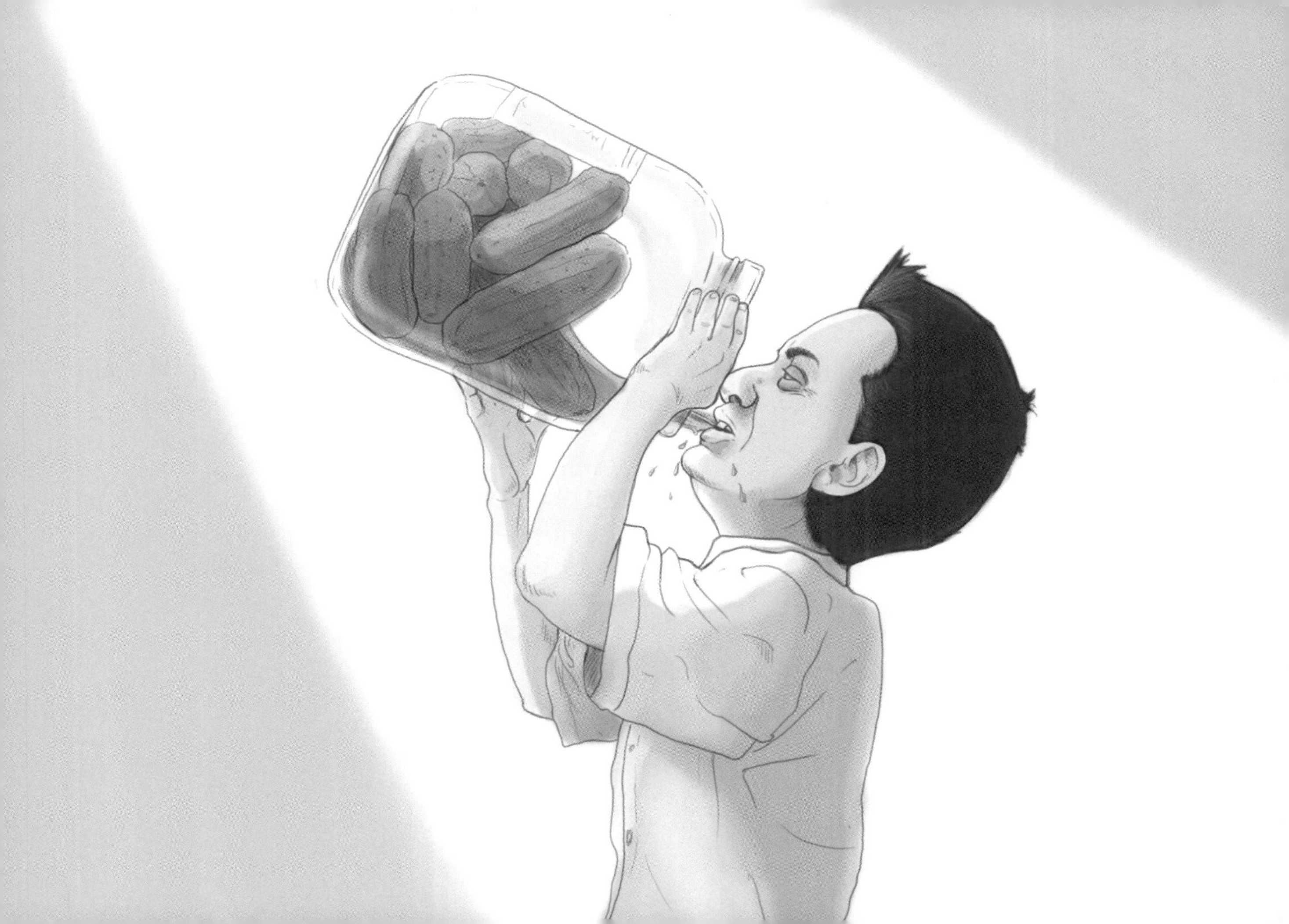

**20 June 2019**
After several rounds of voting and eliminations, Jeremy Hunt and Boris Johnson are the final two candidates remaining in the Conservative Party leadership election.

**TODAY ED MILIBAND...**
spent a good three hours pondering whether he'd rather be eaten alive by a pack of hungry lions OR trampled to death by a herd of angry buffalo.
Final conclusion: both options are horrific.

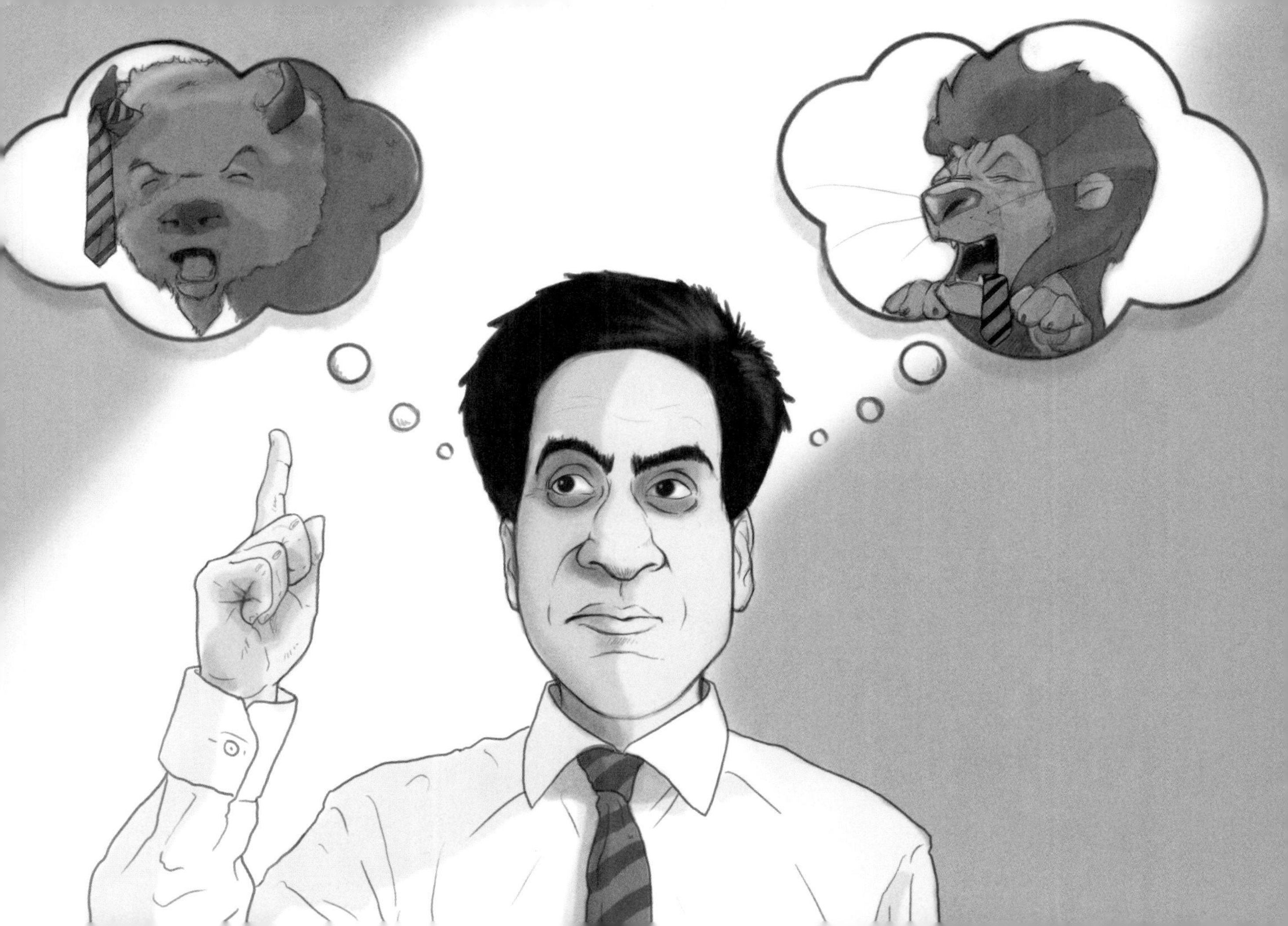

**2 July 2019**
Brexit Party MEPs make headlines for turning their backs on the EU anthem, 'Ode to Joy', during a ceremony to mark the opening of the European Parliament. Liberal Democrat MEPs sport yellow 'Stop Brexit' T-shirts.


**TODAY ED MILIBAND...**
offered to mow his elderly neighbour's lawn. Over seven hours later he finally returned home, having somehow been suckered into doing eleven other gardens on his street.

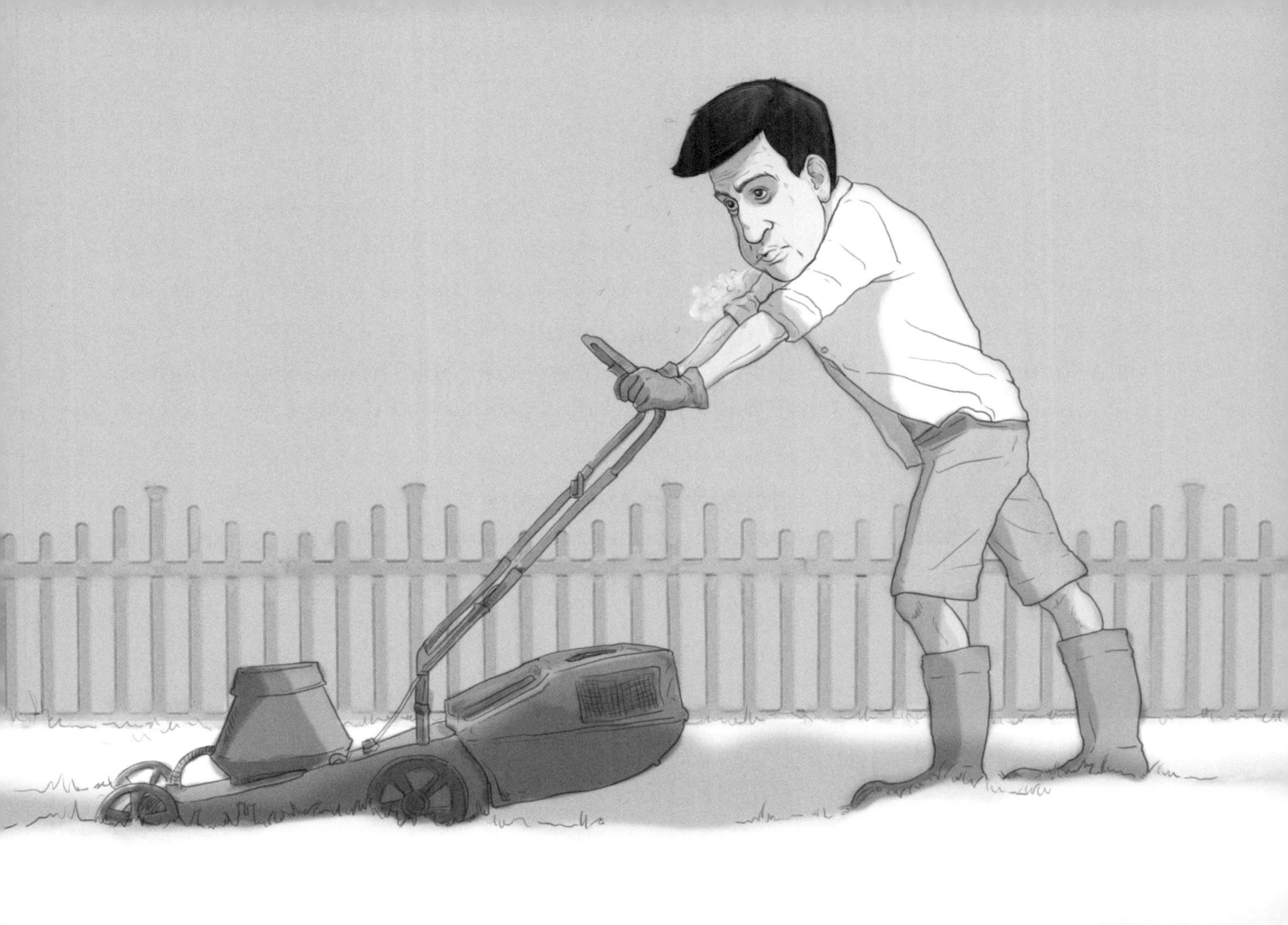

**9 July 2019**
In a series of Tweets, US President Donald Trump criticizes Theresa May's handling of the Brexit negotiations, calling the process 'a disaster!'.


**TODAY ED MILIBAND...**
went to Argos to buy a new paddling pool so he could cool off in the sun, but then fell asleep watching old episodes of *Ready Steady Cook* on YouTube and dropped his iPad in the water. Ruined.

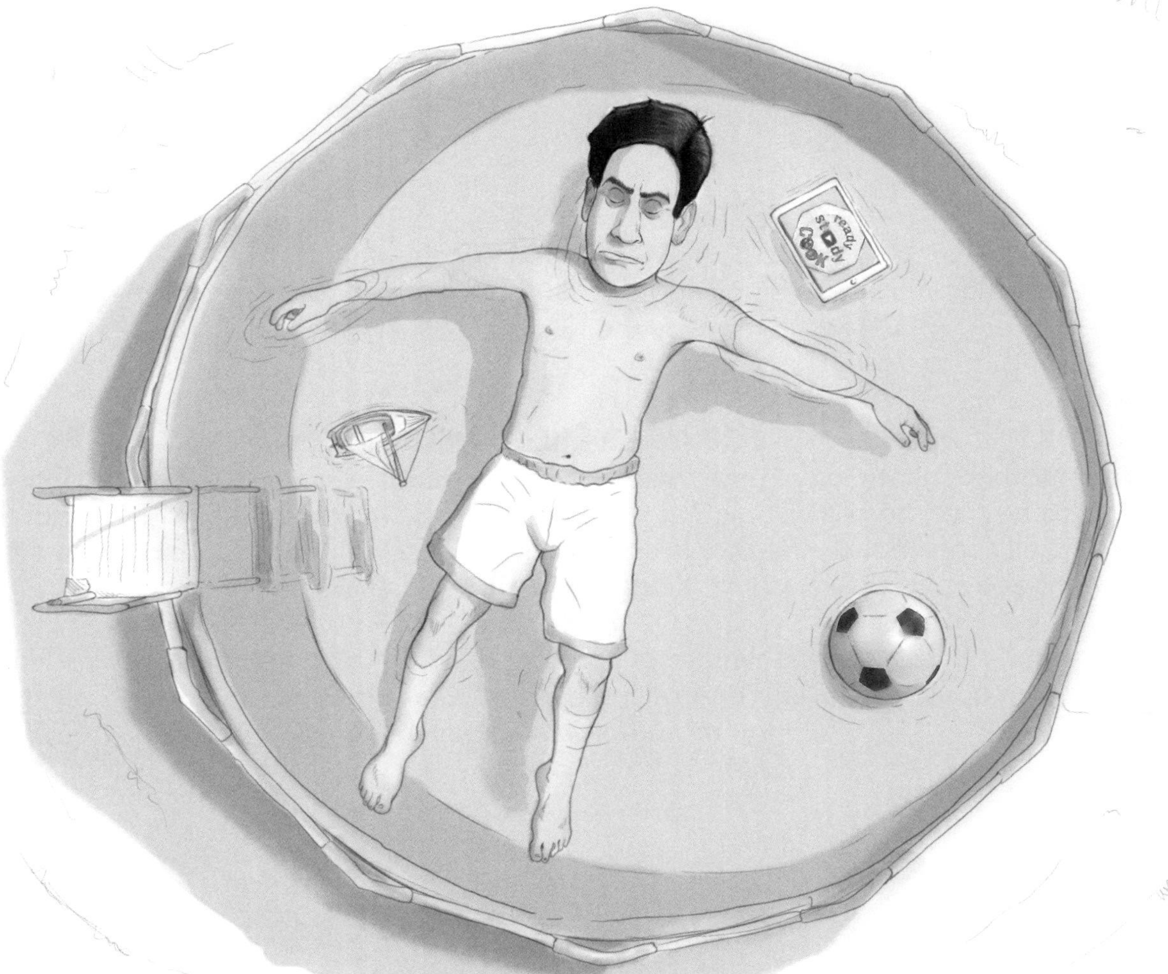
ready

**24 July 2019**
Theresa May officially resigns and Boris Johnson is appointed prime minister
by the Queen.


**TODAY ED MILIBAND...**
lived another chaotic day in the life of Ed Miliband: he was warm and friendly to
everyone he met; he did as much as he could to help anyone who asked; he didn't
take himself too seriously; he didn't have a bad word to say about anybody; and he
went about his business with kindness in his heart and a smile on his face.

And perhaps – in the current climate of division, unrest and sometimes even outright
hostility – we could all do with embracing his particular brand of 'chaos' and being a
bit more like Ed Miliband.

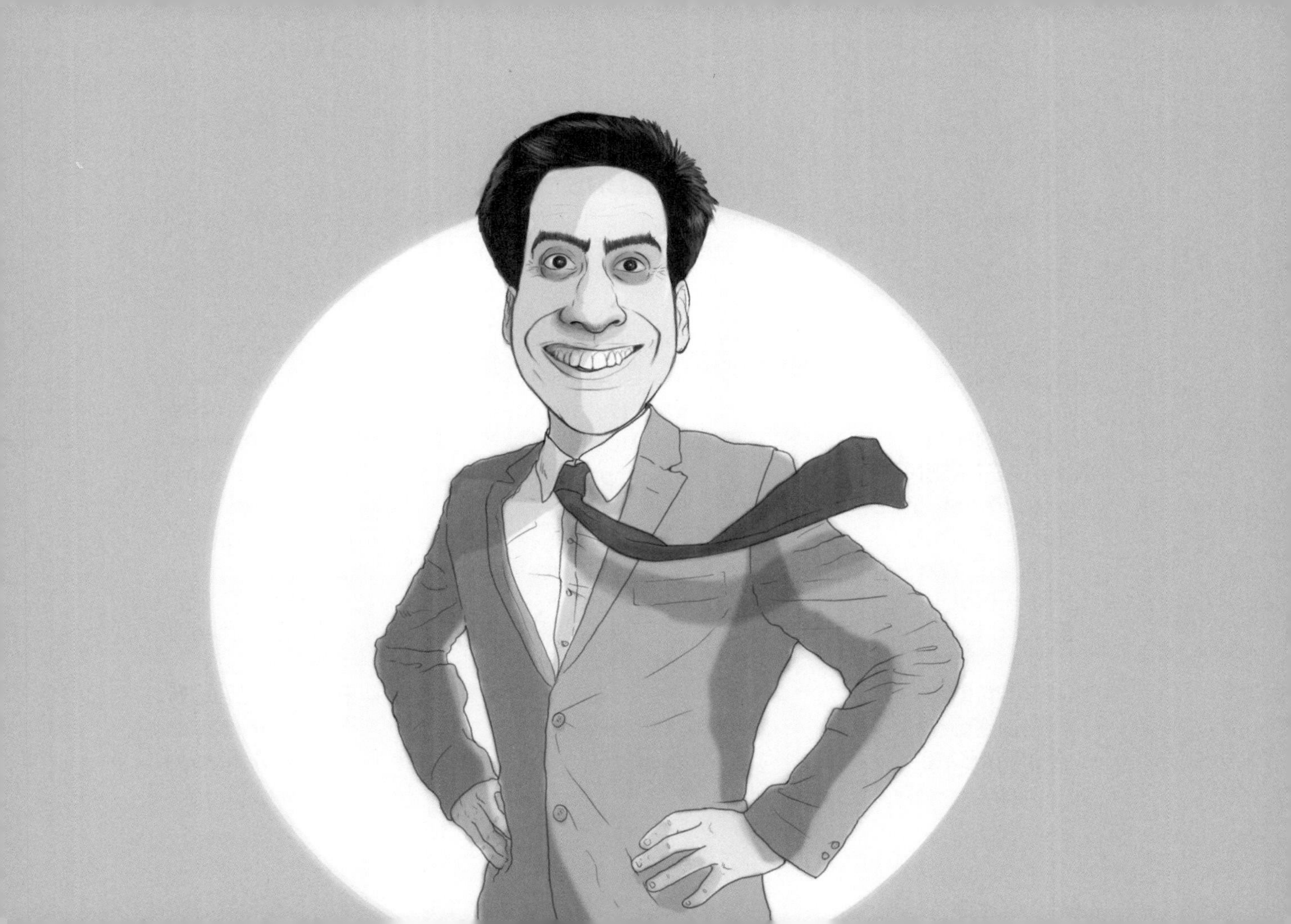

## CREDITS

Trapeze would like to thank everyone at Orion who worked on the publication of *Chaos with Ed Miliband* in the UK:

**EDITOR**
Anna Valentine

**EDITORIAL MANAGEMENT**
Charlie Panayiotou
Jane Hughes
Alice Davis
Tom Noble
Shyam Kumar

**AUDIO**
Paul Stark
Amber Bates

**CONTRACTS**
Anne Goddard
Paul Bulos
Jake Alderson

**DESIGN**
Milligan
The Big Red Illustration Agency
Lucie Stericker
Joanna Ridley
Nick May
Clare Sivell
Helen Ewing

**FINANCE**
Emily-Jane Taylor
Jasdip Nandra
Afeera Ahmed
Elizabeth Beaumont
Sue Baker
Victor Falola

**MARKETING**
Tom Noble

**PRODUCTION**
Katie Horrocks
Fiona McIntosh

PUBLICITY
Francesca Pearce

SALES
Jen Wilson
Victoria Laws
Esther Waters
Rachael Hum
Ellie Kyrke-Smith
Frances Doyle
Ben Goddard
Georgina Cutler
Barbara Ronan
Andrew Hally

Dominic Smith
Maggy Park
Linda McGregor
Sinead White
Jemimah James
Rachael Jones
Jack Dennison
Nigel Andrews
Ian Williamson
Julia Benson
Declan Kyle
Robert Mackenzie

OPERATIONS
Jo Jacobs
Sharon Willis
Lisa Pryde

If you enjoyed *Chaos with Ed Miliband*, why not try the eye-boggling illustrated adventure *Where's Boris?*

## Greetings citizens!

## Can you spot Boris?

In an array of crowded scenes, from zip wires and bikes to Beijing and the Bullingdon Club, search for Boris amongst the masses. Anyone for wiff-waff?

With oodles of in-jokes and bonus material to find, plus cameo appearances from some old chums, this book provides hours of fun for both the lovers and loathers of the blonde-mop-topped phenomenon that is . . . BoJo.

A classic and fun gift book, tracking Boris down around the world will be endless amusement for all the family.

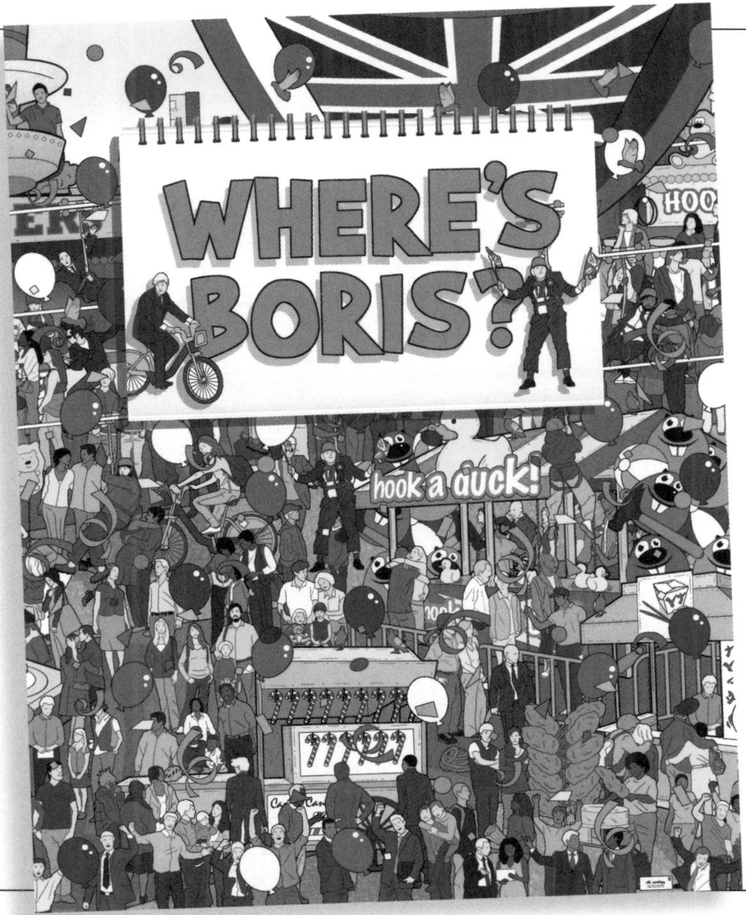

WHERE'S BORIS?
hook a duck!

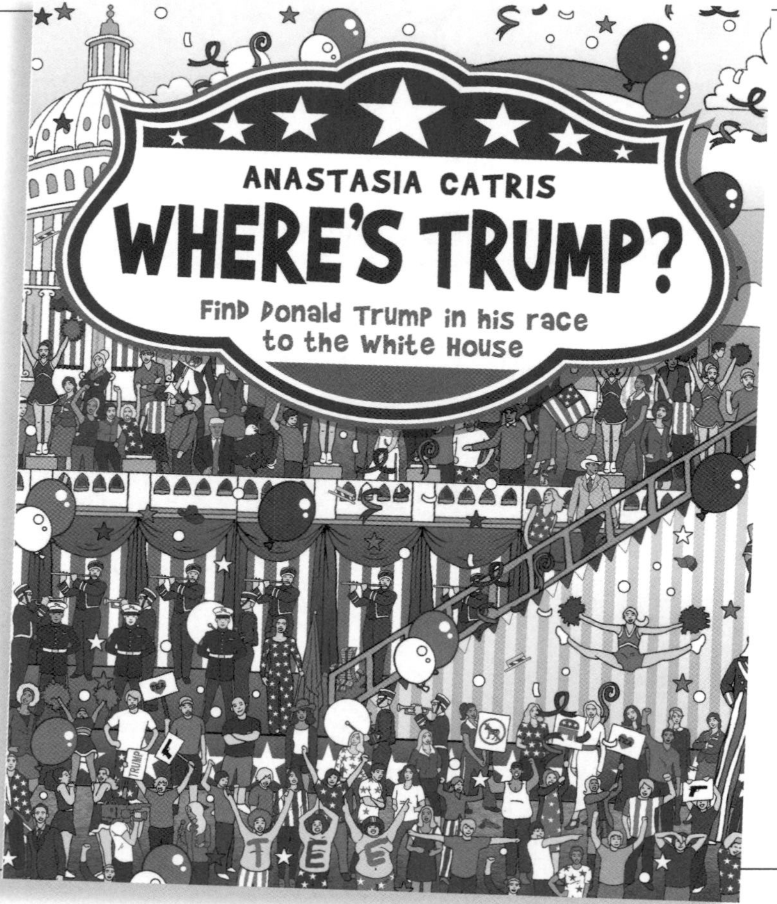
ANASTASIA CATRIS
WHERE'S TRUMP?
Find Donald Trump in his race to the White House

If you still haven't had your fill of political humour then why not also try *Where's Trump?*

## 'Winners aren't losers!'

## Can you spot the Donald?

In an array of crowded scenes, from building a wall around Mexico to carving his face into Mount Rushmore, at a Trump wrestling match, a golf course in Scotland and having fun at a Tea Party rally, search for Donald J. Trump amongst the masses.

With tons of in-jokes and bonus material to find (including Obama's birth certificate and his trademark toupee), plus cameo appearances from Sarah Palin and other high-flying pals, this book provides hours of fun for the haters (and lovers) of the all-American phenomenon that is TRUMP.

A classic and fun gift book, tracking Trump around the world will be endless amusement for all the family.

First published in Great Britain in 2019 by Trapeze,
an imprint of The Orion Publishing Group Ltd
Carmelite House, 50 Victoria Embankment,
London EC4Y 0DZ

An Hachette UK company

1 3 5 7 9 10 8 6 4 2



A CIP catalogue record for this book is available from the British Library.

ISBN (Hardback): 978 1 4091 9596 2
ISBN (ebook): 978 1 4091 9597 9

Printed in Italy

FSC www.fsc.org MIX Paper from responsible sources FSC® C023419

www.orionbooks.co.uk

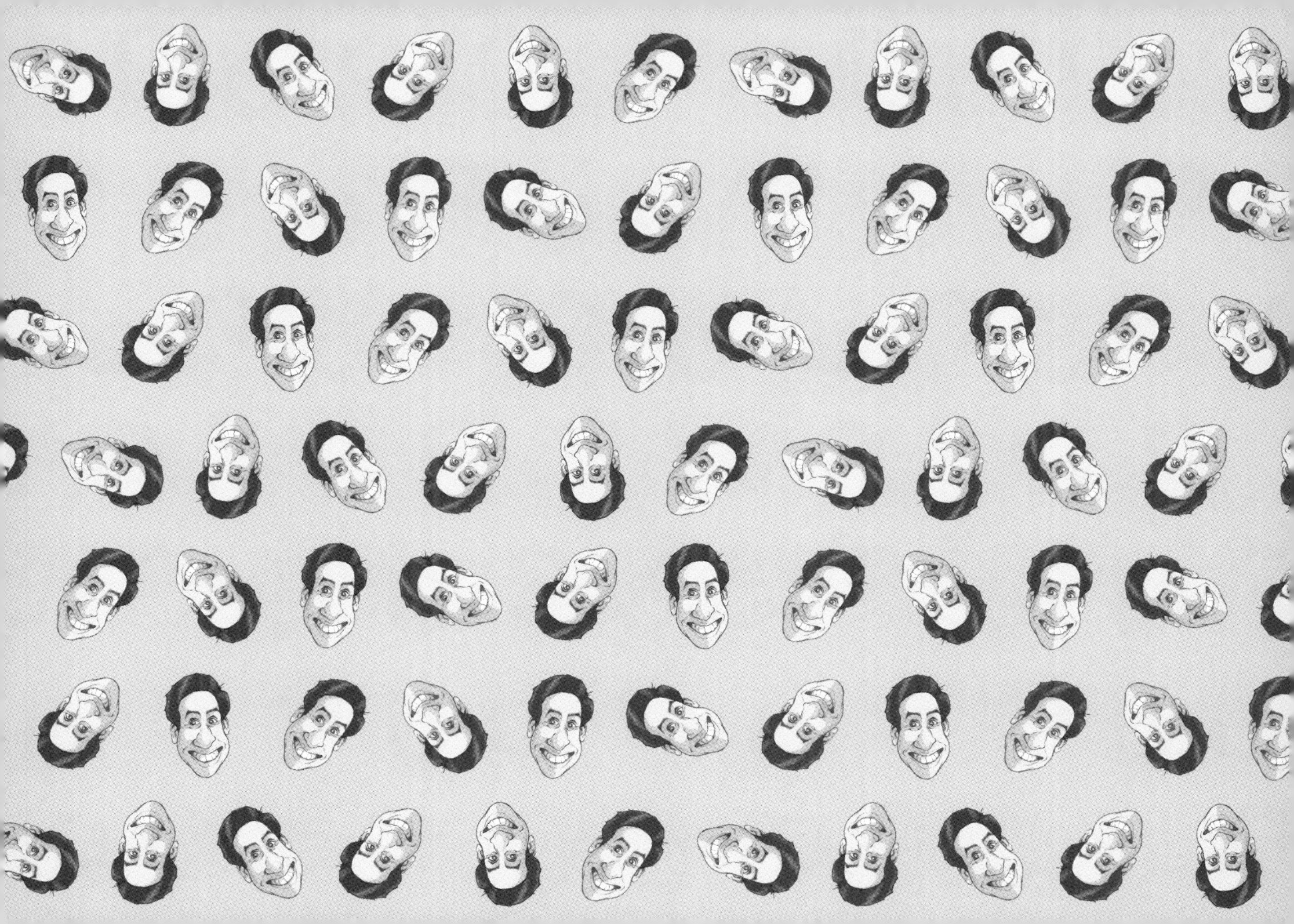

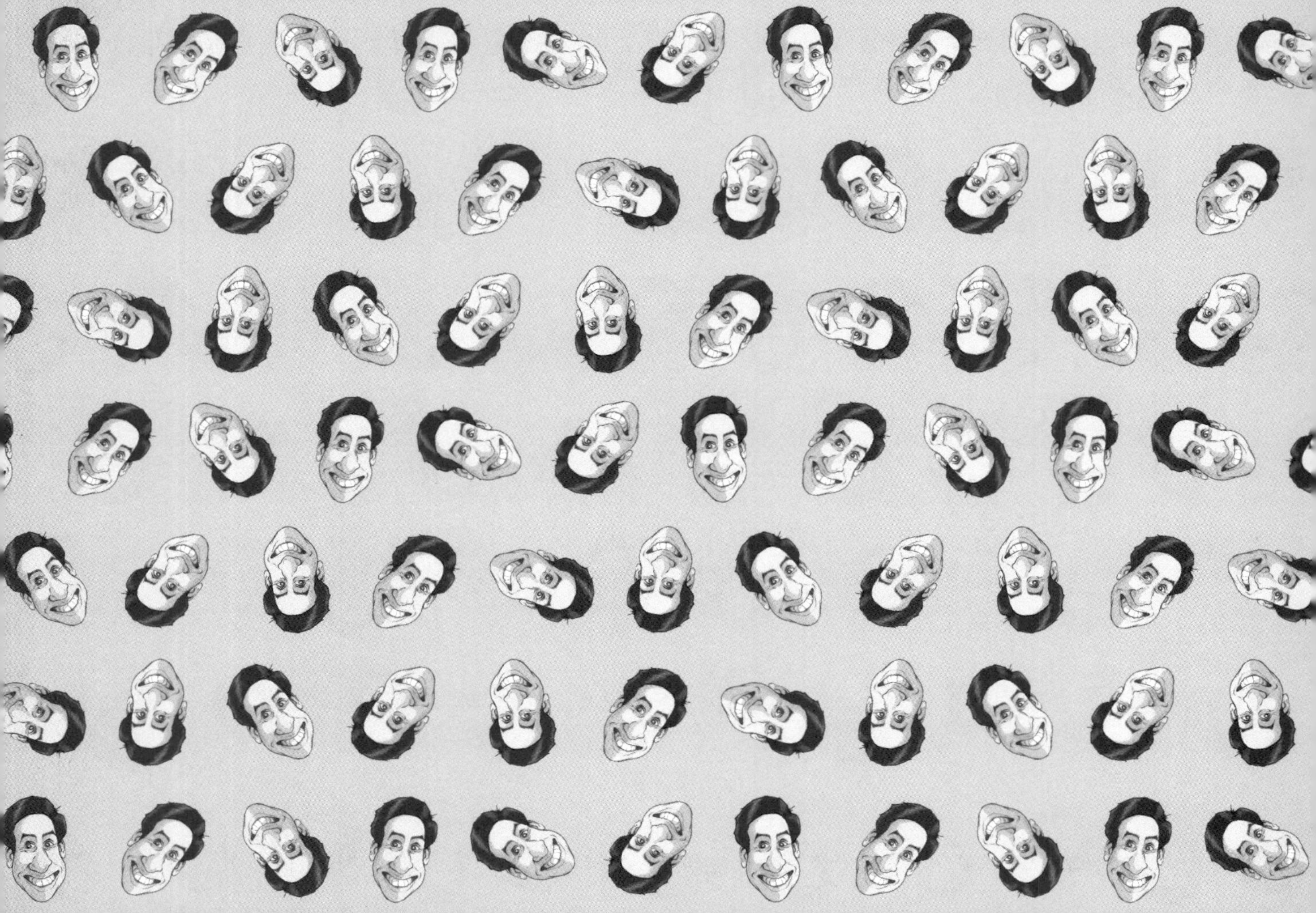